D0595131

Especially for

....

From

....

Date

....

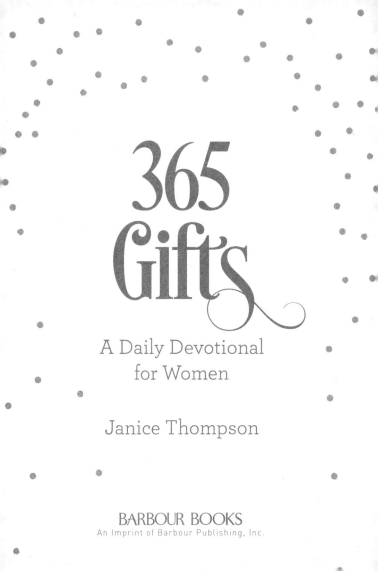

365 Gifts

A Daily Devotional for Women

Janice Thompson

BARBOUR BOOKS
An Imprint of Barbour Publishing, Inc.

© 2018 by Barbour Publishing, Inc.

ISBN 978-1-68322-786-1

Published by Barbour Books, an imprint of Barbour Publishing, Inc., 1810 Barbour Drive, Uhrichsville, Ohio 44683, www.barbourbooks.com

Our mission is to inspire the world with the life-changing message of the Bible.

Member of the
Evangelical Christian
Publishers Association

Printed in the United States of America.

365 Gifts

Every good and perfect gift is from above, coming down from the Father of the heavenly lights, who does not change like shifting shadows.
JAMES 1:17 NIV

Life is filled with gifts—presents to be unwrapped. You find them in a baby's first smile, in a new job opportunity, or in a quiet conversation with a friend. You notice them in a neighbor's greeting, a coworker's pat on the back, and a pastor's sermon. You can't deny them when a Good Samaritan stops to help or a friend lends a helping hand during a time of need.

You've likely experienced hundreds if not thousands of God's gifts over the course of your life. They surprise and delight at every turn. Each is heaven-sent and perfectly timed. They have grown you into the woman you've become.

Those gifts are celebrated in *365 Gifts*. This daily devotional will encourage you to see everyday moments as the treasures they are, gifts from a heavenly Father who adores you. It brings Him great joy to lavish gifts on His children, as you will discover by reading the daily offerings. Each devotion begins with a scripture and ends with a prayer so you can apply what you've read. May you be uplifted, inspired, and encouraged to live every day with a grateful heart for the many blessings God provides.

1

God, the Ultimate Gift

The Lord is not slow in keeping his promise,
as some understand slowness. Instead he is
patient with you, not wanting anyone to perish,
but everyone to come to repentance.
2 PETER 3:9 NIV

How is it possible that the God of the universe, the Creator of everything, decided to enter into relationship with humankind? When you think about the vastness of God—His majesty, His power, His omnipotence—it seems unlikely that He would take the time to speak to you, His creation. Oh, but He created you in His image for relationship with Him. What a thought! He needs you. He wants you. He adores you. Of all the choices He could have made, the Author of all chose to respond in love to humankind, even after we turned our backs on Him. What a gift our Creator is. What a blessing to know we are loved by the almighty Author of everything in spite of anything we might have done. What amazing love!

Thank You, Father, for including me in Your great plan.
When I think about Your greatness, when I contemplate
all You have done to set this world in motion,
I'm awed You would think to include me in
Your plans. I love You, Lord. Amen.

2

Jesus

This is why it says: "When he ascended on high,
he took many captives and gave gifts to his people."
EPHESIANS 4:8 NIV

Have you stopped to ponder the gift of our Savior, Jesus Christ? To leave the throne room of heaven to come to earth as a babe in a manger. . .what a sacrifice! And yet He did it all for you. That's how much He loves you. His ultimate gift—death on the cross—paid for your sins, not just the ones you've already committed but those to come as well. Things you haven't even considered yet. Let that sink in. This love has the power to cleanse, to heal, to reconcile. And it came at such a high cost for Jesus. Ponder His conversation with His Father while in the garden: "If it is not possible for this cup to be taken away unless I drink it, may your will be done" (Matthew 26:42 NIV). Think about His words, laced with agony, as nails held Him bound to the tree: "Father, forgive them, for they do not know what they are doing" (Luke 23:34 NIV). He went through so much, and all for love.

Father, how loved I feel when I think about what Your Son went through for me. He's my Savior, my best friend. He poured Himself out as an offering for me. I can never repay Him, Lord. Praise You for the gift of a Savior! Amen.

3

Holy Spirit

*Peter replied, "Repent and be baptized, every one of you,
in the name of Jesus Christ for the forgiveness of your
sins. And you will receive the gift of the Holy Spirit."*
ACTS 2:38 NIV

It's possible to be surrounded on every side by friends and loved ones and yet feel completely alone. It's a struggle most of us face especially when going through rough seasons that others might not understand. So isn't it amazing to realize that God sent a Helper to live inside of us, a Comforter for our times of need? The Holy Spirit is more than some elusive, ghostlike figure from a fairy tale. He's a gift, One sent from heaven itself. He's here to embolden, to comfort, to heal. He dwells inside you, whispering guidance in your ear while keeping you on the right track. He's an internal GPS system unlike any you could ever purchase. What a gift the Holy Spirit is.

*Father, Your Spirit comforts me when I'm hurting, guides
me when I'm lost, whispers sweet nothings in my ear when
I'm feeling unloved. Where could I go from Your Spirit, Father?
I could hide in the deepest cave and Your Spirit would seek
me out. I'm so grateful for this amazing love. Amen.*

4

The Bible

Your word is a lamp for my feet, a light on my path.
PSALM 119:105 NIV

The Bible is such a gift to believers, isn't it? When you open its pages, it's as if the Creator Himself sits next to you on the sofa and begins to chat. He shares His heart for you, His love, His plan. He points out stories from days gone by of people like Abraham, Moses, and David. When you're hurting, He shares Job's story of overcoming. When you're feeling rejected, He points you to the story of Jacob, rejected by his brothers. Through His Word, God offers guidance and counsel even in your darkest hour. And He's as close as the pages of that precious, holy book. How marvelous to have His words to illuminate each path? Today, pause to thank God for His Word, and then study to show yourself approved, a child of the Most High God thriving on your Father's words.

* * *

God, I'm so grateful to have Your Word. When I think about the people of old, the ones who didn't have access to the Bible, I'm so sad. It breaks my heart to know there are people on this planet right now who still don't have the Bible in their hands. May Your Word spread through every tribe, every nation, Lord. Amen.

5

Salvation

For it is by grace you have been saved, through faith—
and this is not from yourselves, it is the gift of God.
EPHESIANS 2:8 NIV

∼

Salvation—eternal life—is the greatest gift you could ever unwrap. For the believer, it's like Christmas every single day. Bows. Ribbons. Joy. Excitement. The idea that the Creator of the universe would offer mere mortals eternal life is beyond comprehension. To be "saved" is more than just a heart change. It's an *eternity* change. From the moment you asked Jesus to come inside your heart to be the Lord of your life, you were given an eternal perspective. Heaven is now in your sights. It's part of the plan. You're included, redeemed, transformed into Daddy-God's image. All of this came at such a high cost—the blood of Jesus. But He did it all for you.

. . . .

Father, You've saved me! You didn't just pluck me from the
fire; You gave me a new heart and transformed thinking.
You've also given me the promise of heaven, Lord. I'm a new
creation, thanks to the work of Your Son. Praise You! Amen.

6

Living in the Present

*"Therefore do not be anxious, saying, 'What shall
we eat?' or 'What shall we drink?' or 'What shall we wear?'
For the Gentiles seek after all these things, and your heavenly
Father knows that you need them all. But seek first the
kingdom of God and his righteousness, and all these
things will be added to you. Therefore do not be anxious
about tomorrow, for tomorrow will be anxious for
itself. Sufficient for the day is its own trouble."*
MATTHEW 6:31-34 ESV

So many people hover in the past as if afraid to let go and shift
to today. Still others set their sights on tomorrow, wishing
they could somehow avoid the everydayness of what's in front
of them. God has given us the gift of the present. It might be
humdrum, even difficult. But it's still a gift, for it roots and
grounds us in the moment. Lift your head. Look around you.
Let all your anxieties go. Cast them into His hands, and enjoy
today for the gift that it is.

*Father, may I never close my eyes to what You're doing right
here and now. I'm grateful for the gift of this amazing
day, Lord. May I live it fully for You. Amen.*

7

Sense of Wonder

They who dwell in the ends of the earth stand in awe of Your signs; You make the dawn and the sunset shout for joy.
PSALM 65:8 NASB

Oh, to have the wonder of a child, to see every day as a miraculous gift ready to be unwrapped. Can you remember what it felt like to have that sense of childlike anticipation? Do you ever wonder what it would take to glance at the stars, the ocean, fields of bluebonnets and stand in holy amazement once again... to see a miracle every time you look at a newborn's face or a blossoming flower? When your sense of wonder is restored, anticipation builds. God is on the move...and you feel it at every turn. What a blast to have so much to look forward to! God can and will restore your sense of wonder as you draw close to Him. He offers it as a gift, one that continually catches you by surprise and leaves you breathless. What a holy God we serve!

Father, restore my sense of wonder. Give me childlike faith. I want my anticipation to grow as my faith increases. Draw me close, Lord. May I stand in awe of Your majesty as all of creation shouts for joy! Amen.

8

Expectancy

For this reason I remind you to fan into flame the gift of God,
which is in you through the laying on of my hands.
2 TIMOTHY 1:6 NIV

Have you ever considered the notion that expectancy is a gift? We experience it at its height when someone we know is expecting a baby. The process is almost as much fun as the outcome. We rush to the store to purchase goodies in pink or blue, our hearts in a whirl as we think about what the future might hold. We guess the baby's sex, weight, height, and so on. None of these things is known to us in advance. Our expectancy causes us to speculate. That's how it is with our faith walk too. We can't see what's out there, but we speculate that it's going to be something incredible. And why not? We serve a God who loves stirring up expectancy in our hearts. That heightened sense of anticipation brings such a rush as we wait on Him for the big reveal.

Father, I'm looking forward to so many things right now.
You've stirred dreams in my heart and reawakened old
passions. I don't know what the final product will look like,
but I know You're on the move, Lord, and I can't wait! Amen.

9

New Beginnings

*He who was seated on the throne said, "I am making
everything new!" Then he said, "Write this down,
for these words are trustworthy and true."*

REVELATION 21:5 NIV

⬧

Oh, the possibilities when one is given the option of starting
over. What a gift to begin again with a clean, fresh slate. With
all of the mistakes of yesterday behind you, you can step into
a bright new future filled with unlimited opportunities. What a
blessing! What a gift! Maybe you're wondering if such a thing
is possible, if God can really erase the bad things you've done
in the past. He can, and He will if you ask Him to come in and
take charge of your heart. With God leading the way, your entire
perspective will change. You'll have a new way of thinking, which
will lead to brand-new possibilities. God really is making all
things new. That's a promise you can take to the bank.

*Father, thank You for making things new in my heart
and mind. It's miraculous to think You could (and would)
actually erase my sins, wipe my slate clean. I'm so grateful
for the gift of new beginnings, Lord. Amen.*

10

Overcoming Temptation

*No temptation has overtaken you except what is common to
mankind. And God is faithful; he will not let you be tempted
beyond what you can bear. But when you are tempted,
he will also provide a way out so that you can endure it.*
1 CORINTHIANS 10:13 NIV

Don't you wish temptation didn't exist? It's so hard to look the
other way when the very thing you're trying to avoid stares
you in the face, wooing you to touch. Perhaps it's time to look
at temptation as a gift. When you overcome—when you're able
to look the other way—you've come a long way. The old you
would've given in at the first opportunity. These days, even with
temptation tugging away at you, you're able to resist. That's the
Holy Spirit inside you, by the way, giving you the courage and
the wherewithal to say no to the very thing you used to say yes
to all the time. You're a new person now. Temptation has no
hold on you. It's a thing of the past. What a gift!

*Father, I'm so glad that I can say no to temptation. My flesh
is weak. On my own, I could never look the other way.
But with Your Spirit, I am powerful! So I choose to resist,
Lord. Temptation has no hold on me. Amen.*

11

Self-Improvement

I can do all things through him who strengthens me.
PHILIPPIANS 4:13 ESV

We live in a day and age when people are keen on improving themselves. Whether it's diet, exercise, pop psychology, or mental focus, folks everywhere are trying to be a better version of themselves. It's a great idea to improve in areas where you're lacking, but always remember this: where willpower leaves off, God begins. There's only so much you can do on your own. So commit yourself to the Lord, and let Him guide you as improvement begins. And if you flounder (most do, after all), don't beat yourself up. Just begin again and watch as God takes up the slack. What you can't do, He's more than happy to take care of.

Lord, I'm in awe of the transformation taking place in my life since I invited You in. I want to improve—my thoughts, my actions, my reactions—but I recognize I can't do it on my own. Any "self"-improvement really comes down to submitting myself to You, Father. So have Your way in me, I pray. Amen.

12

Transformation

Do not conform to the pattern of this world,
but be transformed by the renewing of your mind.
Then you will be able to test and approve what
God's will is—his good, pleasing and perfect will.
ROMANS 12:2 NIV

Transformation is one of life's finest miracles, and we're privileged to witness it year-round. Winter transforms to spring. Spring shifts to the warm, lazy days of summer and so on. Transformation is equally miraculous when it takes place internally. When our minds are transformed—when our thinking morphs—it's nothing short of a miracle. What a gift, this ability to change. Maybe you're at a place where you think change is impossible. You've tried and failed in the past. You're weary, ready to give up. This time, instead of heading out on your own to take the world on, give it to God. He's the One with the transforming power, after all. He stands ready to lead the way to a new season for you.

Lord, I long to be fully transformed. I'm tired of living in the
dead, dry season of winter. I'm aching for springtime, Father.
Today I offer You my hand so You can lead me there.
I want to be transformed into Your image, Lord. Amen.

13

Goals

Brothers, I do not consider that I have made it my own.
But one thing I do: forgetting what lies behind and straining
forward to what lies ahead, I press on toward the goal for
the prize of the upward call of God in Christ Jesus.
PHILIPPIANS 3:13–14 ESV

Goal-setting is the perfect gift to give yourself not just at the start of a new year but all year long. When you set goals, you're more likely to meet them. This is a biblical principle. Don't build your proverbial house on sinking sand. Anchor it in concrete. Set realistic goals, and then point yourself toward them. Maybe you're not the goal-setting type. Maybe you think you'll start but not finish. Maybe you see yourself as a goal-setting flop. That's okay. God wants you to pick yourself up, brush yourself off, and start the process over again. If you aim at nothing, you will surely hit it. So aim at a closer relationship with Him, and then watch as He helps you meet those goals.

Lord, I've fallen short so many times. I want to be successful,
to set goals and reach them, but I doubt I have the tenacity.
Today I ask You to take over, and help me as only You can.
I point myself at You, Father, so that I can draw close
and lean on Your power. Help me, I pray. Amen.

14

Life

Jesus said to her, "I am the resurrection and the life.
The one who believes in me will live, even though they die;
and whoever lives by believing in me will
never die. Do you believe this?"
JOHN 11:25–26 NIV

Have you ever wished you could have witnessed that spectacular moment when God first breathed life into Adam's lungs? Did they expand and contract with the motion and fluidity of heaven? Did the air itself have power from on high? Did all of creation look on wide-eyed in wonder as the first man drew breath? Was heaven raising a song of celebration, or silent in reverent awe? Perhaps we'll never know, but one thing is sure: even now, God is breathing life—into our bodies, our circumstances, our thought processes. The same creativity that flowed into Adam is rushing into your airways, giving life, power, love. So draw in a deep, heavenly breath, and remember that life is truly a gift.

Thank You, Lord, for the gift of life. You breathed life into me and set all things in motion. You continue to offer life—to my hopes, my dreams, my relationships, and my heart and mind. I praise You for this precious gift, Father. Amen.

15

Joy

May the God of hope fill you with all joy and peace
in believing, so that by the power of the
Holy Spirit you may abound in hope.
ROMANS 15:13 ESV

Joy—that bubbly, bouncy gift that keeps on giving—is straight from heaven. When a friend's words get you giggly, when a child's antics make you smile, you're experiencing a little glimpse of what heaven will be like. Did you know that you can ask God to fill you with joy? He'll do it! Before you know it, you'll spill over onto others you meet. This gift is contagious and has long-term effects. It changes people from the inside out. Best of all, joy leads to a restoration of hope. Maybe you need that today. Maybe you've lost hope. You're ready to give up. Don't! Instead, ask God to fill you with joy, and then watch as He restores your hope in the process. Now *that's* a gift to get excited about!

Father, today I ask You to fill me up from top to bottom with
joy. I want Your version not the world's version. I want to
bubble over with this contagious gift so that all who
come in contact with me will be filled with hope
for the days ahead. Bless You, Lord! Amen.

16

Faith

*Now faith is confidence in what we hope for
and assurance about what we do not see.*
HEBREWS 11:1 NIV

There's something so calming about assurance. When you're sure of a thing, you can relax, be at peace. You don't have to fret or wonder. You know in your knower. Circumstantial evidence doesn't matter. Bumps in the road don't cause you to fret. You have faith that everything will work out fine even when you can't see it with your eyes. *What is faith*, you ask? It's being absolutely, completely, without a doubt sure of what you're hoping for. You're so sure that you'd be willing to bet on it. It's being convinced in your heart of hearts that something you haven't yet seen is going to come to pass. So what are you waiting for? Ask God to pour out the gift of faith, and then trust Him for the impossible!

*Lord, I'm hoping for so many things. I'm not sure my faith
has been strong enough to know without a doubt that
these things will come true, but I'm willing to begin again.
Today I ask that You pour out the gift of faith into my heart
so that I can begin to believe for miracles, Lord. Amen.*

17

Hope

For in this hope we were saved. But hope that is seen is no hope at all. Who hopes for what they already have?
ROMANS 8:24 NIV

It energizes, ignites, lifts, and swells. . .hope. This tiny little word can change a negative attitude to a positive one and set the wheels in motion for a happy, healthy future. When you see life through the lens of hope, you're viewing it from God's perspective. No doom and gloom for you! You have bigger, happier days ahead. Hope has told you so. In fact, it has settled the issue in your heart once and for all. This precious gift—hope—streams down from the heart of your heavenly Father, who wants you to know that He has great things ahead for you. So hang on! Hope is about to take you on a journey you won't soon forget!

Thank You for renewing my hope, Father. I want to be one who lifts her eyes, her heart, her mind to see things the way You do. May I never forget that You are the Author of hope, the One who knows what lies ahead. I'm so excited, Lord. Amen.

18

Restoration

Restore to me the joy of your salvation and
grant me a willing spirit, to sustain me.
PSALM 51:12 NIV

Ever feel like a classic car in need of restoration? Maybe your hubcaps are rusty, or your gas tank is running on empty. Perhaps your outward appearance is out of date, or there are cracks in your interior. Maybe your engine is in need of an overhaul. Truth is, we all need daily restoration and renovation. Sometimes we look at how far we've slipped and wonder if it's possible to get back to where we once were. Instead of focusing on the past, it's more helpful to look to the future and aim yourself at realistic improvements. God is willing to restore our souls, and that's where we must start. What good would it do to improve the exterior of a classic car if you were not fixing the engine first? So what's keeping you? The gift of restoration is waiting!

Father, I know You long to restore all things to Yourself.
Please restore my joy, my hope, my desire to serve You. I long
to receive the gift of restoration in so many areas of my life,
Lord. Let's begin again, You and me. Restore me, I pray. Amen.

19

Provision

*Moreover, when God gives someone wealth and possessions,
and the ability to enjoy them, to accept their lot and
be happy in their toil—this is a gift of God.*
ECCLESIASTES 5:19 NIV

God is an amazing provider. His Word promises that the righteous will never be forsaken, and their children won't have to beg for bread. His provision is such a gift, one He longs to give. He provides food to the hungry, clothes for the naked, and shelter for the homeless. He gives hope to the hopeless, joy to the joyless, and peace to the one in agony. Whatever you're lacking, that's what He longs to provide. So what are you lacking today? What holes need to be filled? A job? Health? Food for your family? A new car? A lower electric bill? A reduced mortgage? Be specific when you pray, and ask your Father God to make provision. Chances are pretty good that He's already working on it.

*Father, You want to fill all the holes in my life. You want to
make provision in every area. How You love me, Lord! I open
myself up to Your fullness. Fill every hole. Provide where
there is lack. I trust You to meet every need, Lord. Amen.*

20

Vision

There is surely a future hope for you,
and your hope will not be cut off.
PROVERBS 23:18 NIV

All of the human senses are a gift, but vision is near the top of the list. Our eyes show us more than just the brilliant blue sky or the pink azaleas. They home in on the details of a bumble-bee's stripes and a lizard's tail, a sunset's brilliant colors, or a baby's first tooth. Our sight gives us courage to step ahead on the path and warns us when we're about to land in a pothole. It sees in the peripheral too, showing us incoming trouble on the right or left. Today, why not pause and ask God to increase your spiritual vision. He longs to give you the ability to see through His eyes. He wants you to see the future with hopeful eyes, believing for the miraculous. He also wants to increase your vision to see what the enemy is up to. (The enemy's trying to throw you off course, so look out!) Most of all, He wants you to see how dearly you are loved.

Father, increase my spiritual vision, I pray. Open my eyes that I may see as You do. I want to know how to minister to people around me. I want to be aware of the enemy's schemes. Most of all, I long to know and love You more, Lord. Amen.

21

Home

When Naomi heard in Moab that the LORD had come to the aid of his people by providing food for them, she and her daughters-in-law prepared to return home from there.
RUTH 1:6 NIV

Home. There's no place like it. It's more than just the location where you hang your hat; it's where shoulders are unburdened, hearts are reinvigorated, and consciences are cleared. It's where you receive sustenance, find rest, and grow relationships. The sense of comfort that takes place inside your own home can't be matched. You won't find it in any other place. So throw open the front door. Step inside. Take a deep breath. Feel the comfort of acceptance. You're home, child. You're home.

Father, I love my physical home, but I also love spending time with You. I truly feel like I'm finally at home when I'm in Your presence. You feed me, give me rest, and help me grow in my relationship with You and others. You accept me, usher me through the door, and wrap me in Your arms. I'm at home with You, Daddy-God, and I'm so happy! Amen.

22

Friends

*There are "friends" who destroy each other,
but a real friend sticks closer than a brother.*
PROVERBS 18:24 NLT

Ah, the inner circle! How good and lovely to dwell in community—surrounded by a tight-knit group of people who have your back. They give you the "what for" when you need it, a swift kick when the situation calls for it, and a shoulder to cry on when your heart is heavy. What a gift these precious people are! Maybe you're feeling friendless today. Perhaps situations have blown out of proportion or feelings are hurt. God longs to restore, to heal, to breathe new life into friendships. Today, offer Him that part of your life, and then watch as He fills the holes in your heart with friends, old and new.

Lord, I long for godly friends. I want to love and be loved by others. Show me which of my current friendships are meant to be long term and which ones need to fall by the wayside. Bring new friends into my life, I pray, and help me to be the best possible friend to others. Amen.

23

Spiritual Gifts

*I long to see you so that I may impart to you
some spiritual gift to make you strong.*
ROMANS 1:11 NIV

Have you unwrapped your gifts today? The Lord has special packages with your name on them. They're waiting to be opened. Each has a special purpose and, perhaps, a special season of use. What will you find once the ribbon and paper are torn away. . . discernment? The gift of healing? A word of knowledge to lift someone's heart? The gift of prophecy, perhaps? Teaching? Encouragement? Administration? Take the time to read God's Word. Discover the various spiritual gifts He has to offer, and then open yourself to the possibilities. It's time to open those presents and peek inside!

*Lord, I don't know which of the spiritual gifts are mine for the
taking. Sometimes I think it's one thing; other times I think it's
another. Today I open myself as a vessel and ask You to
pour Your gifts inside. Use me to reach others, I pray,
as I submit to the flow of Your gifts through me. Amen.*

24

Worship

*On coming to the house, they saw the child with his
mother Mary, and they bowed down and worshiped him.
Then they opened their treasures and presented
him with gifts of gold, frankincense and myrrh.*
MATTHEW 2:11 NIV

Some think of worship as a song service in church, hands lifted in praise, voices ringing out with the praises of God. This is one form of worship, but there are so many more, and each is a gift. Loving others is an act of service. So is giving. Caring for those in need. You worship God when you treat others with respect, when you honor your parents (no matter their age), and when you raise your children to love Him. Caring for widows and orphans is an act of worship, as is volunteering to work in children's church or singing in the choir. There are so many ways you can worship the Lord, but ultimately it comes down to loving Him. Pouring out your love to Him is the ultimate act of worship.

*Lord, I long to worship You in every area of my life—
my relationships, my work, my giving, my church life. I'm on
a learning curve, Father, so show me as we move forward in
our relationship how to bring honor to Your name. Amen.*

25

Accountability Partners

Iron sharpens iron, and one man sharpens another.
PROVERBS 27:17 ESV

She keeps you walking the straight and narrow. She dares to tell you the truth even when no one else will. She's your accountability partner, and she's a gift straight from heaven. With her arm firmly linked in yours, you have a better chance of slaying giants, conquering demons, and growing into the woman you were created to be. Sure, she doesn't let you get away with much. You're tough on her too. But isn't that the point? You agreed to take on the position so that iron could sharpen iron, so that you could both grow in Christ. So take the lumps even if she doesn't dish them out the way you'd hoped. Together, you're growing into mighty women of God.

Father, thank You for placing women in my life who will sharpen me. They don't let me get away with much, but I love them anyway. I want to be all You want me to be, Lord, even if the growing process is tough at times. I submit myself to it. Amen.

26

Self-Reliance

Finally, be strong in the Lord and in the strength of his might.
EPHESIANS 6:10 ESV

Most Christians shy away from "self"-anything. They argue that any strength they have comes from God, and that's true. But He gifted us with amazing minds and hearts as well as the ability to fend for ourselves, so it's important to recognize the fact that our "self" has power too. We are created in His image, after all. Taking care of yourself, relying upon yourself for the most basic things in life, is a learned gift—one the Lord takes seriously. He longs to grow His kids into mighty men and women. So let Him finish the work He has started in you. You're growing even now!

Thank You, Lord, for the gift of self-reliance. I want to be responsible in all areas of my life. I don't want to be guilty of leaning on others too much or demanding attention. I want to be responsible, Father. Thank You for showing me how. Amen.

27

Uprightness

For the Lord God is a sun and shield; the Lord bestows favor and honor. No good thing does he withhold from those who walk uprightly.
PSALM 84:11 ESV

Holiness. Integrity. Uprightness. These are all words used to describe followers of Christ. Sure, we don't always feel holy. We don't always choose integrity. And we don't walk uprightly all of the time. Sometimes we sink down to the depths. We forget to care. Then God, with His amazing grace, reminds us that any uprightness, any holiness, comes from Him. We don't have to work for it. We can't manufacture it. We don't even have to worry about whether or not we're getting things right. We simply have to draw near to the Father and trust His work in us. He is working, you know. Even now. And this precious gift—uprightness—is one you can count on as His work is perfected in you.

Lord, thank You for the reminder that I don't have to work harder to be holy or upright. Nothing I do will win brownie points with You, Father. Anything good in me comes from You, a gift I will never take for granted. Thank You, Lord! Amen.

28

Dreams

" 'In the last days, God says, I will pour out my Spirit on all people. Your sons and daughters will prophesy, your young men will see visions, and your old men will dream dreams.' "
ACTS 2:17 NIV

God has gifted all of his kids (young and old) with hopes and dreams. He's an amazing dream-giver. No doubt you've spent hours thinking and dreaming about what you want to do or where you want to go. The ability to see your future as a positive, hopeful place is truly a gift. God is a dreamer too. He dreamed up you. . .and your amazing friends, family members, and loved ones. He wants you to dream big like He does. You're created in His image, after all. So what are your hopes and dreams at the beginning of this New Year? Where do you see the road taking you? Put your hand in His and begin to dream in color, and then watch as that dream unfolds!

Father, I want to dream big like You do. You're the ultimate source of creativity, and I long to tap into that as I spin visions and dreams into place. What lies ahead? I'm not sure, but I know it's going to be amazing, Lord, because You'll be right there in the center of it all! Amen.

29

Boundaries

For each will have to bear his own load.
GALATIANS 6:5 ESV

Boundaries are a safety net. They protect you from being taken advantage of. They provide comfort, courage, and care. Best of all, they keep others from robbing you of your time, talents, and treasures. The ability to put boundaries in place comes from the Lord. It doesn't always feel good. Using the word *no* doesn't come easily to some people. But, like anything else in life, the more you use it, the easier it gets. So take a good look at your life today. What areas need boundary lines? Is someone draining you of your time, demanding too much attention? Do you need to utilize the word *no* when that next text or phone call comes? Go ahead and practice ahead of time. Look in the mirror, and say it with gusto: "No. Nope. Can't do it. Sorry, but not this time." There, doesn't that feel good?

I'm drawing boundary lines, God. You'll have to help me. It won't be easy, especially with a couple people who've tugged on my heartstrings over the years. But I can do it with Your help, Father. Thank You in advance. Amen.

30

Sanctity of Life

For You formed my inward parts;
You wove me in my mother's womb.
PSALM 139:13 NASB

When God breathes life into a living thing, a miracle takes place. Out of nothing comes something! Remarkable, if you think about it. It's so fascinating to think He cares about even the little ones who aren't born yet. If He took the time to form children in the womb—to weave them together as an artist weaves a tapestry—then He must care deeply about what happens to them in that holy place. Deep within a mother's womb, the child celebrates the greatest gift of all—life. And it's a gift we must all fight to preserve.

Father, thank You for the reminder that unborn children are precious to You. Their lives matter so deeply. I praise You for weaving me together in my mother's womb all those years ago. I'm fearfully and wonderfully made, Lord! Help me see that these little ones are destined for greatness, Lord. Amen.

31

Health

*Dear friend, I pray that you may enjoy good health
and that all may go well with you, even as
your soul is getting along well.*
3 John 1:2 niv

~⚬~

May we never take for granted the gift of health. To be of sound mind and body is such a gift. That's why we work so hard to rest, eat the right foods, and manage stress, so we might enjoy wellness. When we do walk through seasons of illness, God walks with us. It's evident from today's scripture that the Lord cares a great deal about our physical well-being. It brings such comfort to know He longs for all to go well with us and that we might be in good health. Today, pause and thank the Lord for the gift of health. No matter where you are in your journey, your heavenly Father cares.

Lord, thank You for caring about my health. Show me how to take the best possible care of myself so that I can share in the beauty of this life for years to come. Praise You, Father. Amen.

32

Love

Now eagerly desire the greater gifts.
And yet I will show you the most excellent way.
1 CORINTHIANS 12:31 NIV

Look up the word *love* in the dictionary, and you'll find a variety of definitions. To some, it's a feeling that floats over you, almost transcendent and uncontrollable. To others, it's an action—caring for others even when they don't deserve it. Some would even say love is neither feeling nor action, that it simply doesn't exist, that it's something romance writers have cooked up to sell books or movie networks have dreamed up to sell movies. What do you say about love? Do you see it for what it is. . .a gift straight from heaven? Love intervened in your life when you didn't deserve it. It healed your broken heart. It came as a babe in a manger and died on a cross so that you could have eternal life. Love, it turns out, is a Savior, and Jesus is His name.

Lord, You are love. You have dispelled every myth, broken every lie. You came, You saw, You gave. . .and I've been the recipient of Your love. Oh, how it has changed my life, this amazing love! Praise You, Father. Amen.

33

Clothing

But if we have food and clothing,
we will be content with that.
1 TIMOTHY 6:8 NIV

～

If you're like most, your closet is overflowing with clothes for all seasons. Some fit beautifully. Others, not so much. They hang there, taunting you, begging you to lose those last fifteen pounds. Still others are out of fashion. Their shoulder pads shout, "Remember the eighties?" or "That color went out twenty years ago!" Oh, but isn't it lovely to have what you need to cover the body God gave you? Clothes are a gift—a colorful, straitlaced or flouncy gift. They hint at your personality (Wow, she's bright!) and provide an external hint of who you are as a person. They are the cover of the book that is you. So instead of bemoaning all of the clothes that don't fit, thank the Lord for His provision, and wear those clothes with style!

. . . .

Father, thank You for providing me with the things I need
to survive—food, clothes, and shelter. Today I'm especially
grateful for a filled closet and drawers that are overflowing
with clothes, both old and new. Praise You for giving me
all I need and more. I'm so grateful, Lord. Amen.

34

Heartbreaks

He heals the brokenhearted and binds up their wounds.
PSALM 147:3 ESV

Chances are you've never considered heartbreak a gift. To you, it feels like the end of everything good. Oh, but it can be a gift if you change your perspective a bit! Heartbreak always takes you someplace new. If you've never known the pain of heartbreak, you'll never fully understand the joy on the other side. Sloshing through a season of being brokenhearted can take a toll on your emotions and health, but standing whole and healed once the heart has been mended by the King of kings? Priceless. Every broken place has been super-glued back together, stronger than ever. Every hole, filled. If you happen to be muddling your way through the pain right now, lift your head. Joy is coming in the morning, and you will be stronger than you've ever been.

Lord, only You can mend a broken heart. I know You understand what it feels like because You watched Your children turn on Jesus—betraying, beating, and even murdering Him. How that must have grieved Your heart. Thank You for the joy that comes after the pain. I'm looking forward to that, Father. Amen.

35

Snow

"He says to the snow, 'Fall on the earth,'
and to the rain shower, 'Be a mighty downpour.' "
JOB 37:6 NIV

Glistening. White. Crystals so intricately detailed, each one could be immortalized in an art gallery. Featherlight, these snowflakes tumble from the sky above, a reminder of freshness, beauty, and purity. (There's a reason the phrase "white as the driven snow" has lasted this long.) God sends snow as a gift, a reminder that He still controls both the heavens and the earth. So what's holding you back? Get out there and enjoy the day. Build a snowman. Go sledding. Enjoy the gift before the temperatures rise and cause it to melt.

Father, thank You for the reminder that heaven and earth
are fully under Your control. You bring the rain, the sunshine,
the snow. You dry the land in due season. I'm so grateful
that I don't have to wonder or be afraid with seasonal
changes, Lord. You will take care of us winter, spring,
summer, or fall. Praise You for that! Amen.

36

Valentines

Place me like a seal over your heart, like a seal on your arm;
for love is as strong as death, its jealousy unyielding as the
grave. It burns like blazing fire, like a mighty flame.
SONG OF SOLOMON 8:6 NIV

Those adorable little cards, all pink and white and red, covered
in tiny foil hearts and mushy sentiments—how we love them.
An elementary schoolchild's valentine box is a sign of all that's
right with the world, people loving people no matter their differences. And there's something rather magical about the process
of choosing a particular card to give to that certain someone
you have your eye on. How delightful! How precious. Perhaps
this notion of blessing others with sweet words comes straight
from the Lord Himself. He adores us, after all. Even now He's
singing a love song over you. What an amazing valentine He is!

Lord, You are the ultimate valentine. You know just what to
say to win my heart, Father. You've given me Your Word as a
gift. It's better than any card I could ever receive and filled
with more words of love than anyone could ever speak over
me. Oh, how I love You, Lord. Thank You for the reminder
of the depth of Your love for me. Amen.

37

Hot Chocolate

You will increase my greatness and comfort me again.
PSALM 71:21 ESV

It's just the thing to warm you on a bitterly cold day—a luscious, whipped-cream-topped mug of hot chocolate. There's something so comforting about the taste and texture of this creamy beverage. The cocoa offers satisfaction, and the warmth seems to go all the way to the bones. There's no way you can sip hot chocolate and remain in a bad mood, especially if you throw a few mini-marshmallows on top. It will leave you smiling and sighing every single time. So what are you waiting for? Grab your favorite mug. You know the one. Heat up the kettle and grab the bag of marshmallows. It's time to take the chill off. Have some cocoa to drink!

Lord, thank You for comfort foods and drinks like hot chocolate. Life leaves me feeling so cold sometimes, but there are days when a simple cup of cocoa can make all the difference. Today is one of those days, Father. So let me grab my cup, and I'll be back for a little chat. Amen.

38

Warm Slippers

My eyes fail, looking for your promise; I say,
"When will you comfort me?"
PSALM 119:82 NIV

They warm your feet on a chilly winter's night and bring a sense of coziness at once. They provide traction against the slippery floor with the little grippers on the bottom. Those warm, fuzzy slippers represent more than just a common foot covering; they're a sign to all that you're off the clock. . .no work going on here. I'm lounging, thank you very much. Don't ask me to walk any great distances or perform any tasks. Sorry, no can do. These shoes aren't made for walking; they're made for cozying up to a fireplace and sipping a cup of tea while reading a good book. Ah, the joy of resting with your slippered feet up! So why wait? Grab your slippers and settle in!

Father, I love those special wintry days when I'm able to stay
inside and relax with a good book. Thank You for the gift of
coziness that comes with slippers, hot tea, and a cozy chair.
I'm so grateful for the comforts of home, Lord. Amen.

39

God's Goodness

If you, then, though you are evil, know how to give good
gifts to your children, how much more will your Father
in heaven give good gifts to those who ask him!
MATTHEW 7:11 NIV

Aren't you glad you don't always get what you deserve? The goodness of God serves as a reminder that He's taken the price for us, that He sees us as purified, wiped clean by the sacrifice of His Son. It's the goodness of God that leads us to repentance. Because He's good, we know we can trust Him. And because we can trust Him, we're more willing to admit our flaws. That's what our relationship is all about, after all. He loves us, we love Him. . . and it all starts with His goodness. Have you witnessed the Father's goodness in your life firsthand? If so, why not spend some time thanking Him for all He's done. He's worthy of your praise, and not just for the things He's done but for who He is.

Thank You for Your goodness, Lord! I don't always
deserve it, but You continue to give. What a
loving Father You are. I'm so grateful. Amen.

40

Spouse/Future Spouse

Therefore a man shall leave his father and his mother and hold fast to his wife, and they shall become one flesh.
GENESIS 2:24 ESV

They're all around you. . .married people. Maybe you're one of them, blissfully in love in a happily-ever-after relationship. Or maybe you're single, wishing to be married. You're getting a little tired of hunting for Prince Charming. You're wondering if your future spouse is even out there and, if he is, what's taking him so long to find his way to you. Instead of giving up, begin to praise the Lord now for the work that He's doing in the heart and mind of the one you will one day love. Won't it be fun a few years from now to look back and say, "Hey, I prayed for you before I even knew you!" So what's holding you back? Go ahead. Plant those seeds so they can blossom and grow.

Lord, I'll admit I'm not very patient when it comes to waiting for Mr. Right. I find myself distracted, wanting to rush the process. Thank You for the reminder that I can begin to plant seeds into this future relationship by praying even now. Amen.

41

Mistakes

*Indeed, we all make many mistakes. For if we could control
our tongues, we would be perfect and could also
control ourselves in every other way.*
JAMES 3:2 NLT

"Oops! Sorry about that! Can I have a do-over? Pretty please?"
Life offers continual opportunities to get it wrong, doesn't it?
Just about the time you think you're doing well. . .*bam!* Another
oops moment. So you pick yourself up and start over again,
apologizing when necessary and promising yourself you'll do
better next time. And there will always be a next time. Mistakes
are, after all, one of God's gifts to us to prove that we must rely
on Him—not ourselves. They also teach us grace and mercy.
So what will you do next time? Here's a little tip: instead of
looking back over your shoulder, learn from the experience,
thank God for the gift of starting over, and hit the road with
your head held high.

*Lord, I make so many mistakes. Sometimes I embarrass
myself. I want so desperately to get it right all the time,
but I just can't. Today I'm pausing to thank You for grace.
You offer it so willingly, even when I mess up big-time.
I'm grateful for Your mercy, Father. Amen.*

42

Parents

Children, obey your parents in the Lord, for this is right.
"Honor your father and mother"—which is the first
commandment with a promise—"so that it may go well
with you and that you may enjoy long life on the earth."
Fathers, do not exasperate your children;
instead, bring them up in the training
and instruction of the Lord.
EPHESIANS 6:1–4 NIV

Mom. Pop. Mother. Father. Mama. Daddy. Whatever you choose to call them, they are the ones who gave you life and cared for your needs while growing up. Your parents would probably argue that you were a gift to them—and you were—but the same is true in reverse. They have been a blessing in your life as well. After all, they saw you through your teen years! They worked long, hard hours to shape you into the person you've become, and often without thanks. So pause for a moment today and praise God for the ones who brought you into this world. What a gift your parents have been!

Lord, I'm so grateful for my mom and dad. They cared for my
needs and saw me through so many hard times. May I never
forget that they are a gift from You, Father. Amen.

43

Neighbors

*For the entire law is fulfilled in keeping this one
command: "Love your neighbor as yourself."*
GALATIANS 5:14 NIV

They wave to you from across the lawn, water your yard when you're out of town, and bring food when you're sick or someone in the family has passed away. Neighbors are the real deal. They see you at your best (when you win yard of the month) and your worst (when your dog keeps them awake at night). They fuss at you when your house needs painting and pat you on the back when you get a job promotion. Of course, the word *neighbor* doesn't just signify someone who lives nearby. God has filled your life with neighborly folk. The man who works in the gas station. The checkout lady at the supermarket. The boy who delivers your paper. All of these and more fall into the category of neighbor. And what a gift they are, these amazing people!

* *

*Father, thank You for surrounding me with people who
care. I want to be a good neighbor to everyone I meet,
both near and far. May I truly learn to love
my neighbor as myself, Lord. Amen.*

44

Balance

But seek first the kingdom of God and his righteousness,
and all these things will be added to you.
MATTHEW 6:33 ESV

Do you ever feel as if you're walking a tightrope far above the crowd, arms loaded down with superfluous stuff? Onlookers cheer when you take cautious steps, then gasp in fear when you teeter and wobble. You lose your grip on a couple of objects, and they hurl to the ground below, creating a mess. Today, as you think about all of the many tasks you've taken on, as you ponder your journey across the tightrope of life, remember that balance is a gift. When your arms are overloaded, you stand a greater chance of falling. What can you let go of today? Lay it down, and trust that the Lord will take care of it for you. Then focus on the journey so that you can stay upright all the way.

Lord, I confess I often take on too much. I convince myself that I can handle more than others can, that I'm wired differently. But I get burned out and wonder why I feel overwhelmed. Thank You for the reminder that I'm designed to walk in balance. Show me what I can lay down today, Father. I choose to do so that I might walk uprightly. Amen.

45

Sensitivity

Live in harmony with one another. Do not be proud,
but be willing to associate with people of low
position. Do not be conceited.
ROMANS 12:16 NIV

You can tell by looking at her that she's in a rough spot. You pick up on the red-rimmed eyes and downcast expression. She's trying hard to cover up the pain, but it's not hidden to you. You have the gift of sensitivity, so you move in with tender care, offering a shoulder she can lean on, an ear that will listen. She takes you up on that offer and pours out her heart. That sensitive spirit of yours is a gift both to others and yourself. It's what sets you apart from so many who don't seem to notice when folks around them are hurting. You notice though. And you feel drawn to help. Your heart is tender and your actions laced with compassion and love.

Thank You for opening my eyes to see, Lord. I don't want to
rush by those in need. May my spirit always be sensitive
to the cries of those around me that I might be
Your hands, Your feet to a hurting world. Amen.

46

Reverence

Submit to one another out of reverence for Christ.
EPHESIANS 5:21 NIV

❧

Reverence. A deep, abiding respect. Showing honor or regard. These are just a few of the definitions of the word *reverence*. It's wonderful to show someone this sort of respect (and wonderful to be treated with respect as well), but it's even greater to show it to the One who is most worthy. God deserves our utmost, our highest. We offer Him reverence as a gift straight from the heart. We don't revere Him because of the things He does for us. We show Him honor simply because of who He is. He's the King of kings and Lord of lords, after all. Creator of all. Healer. Victor. Blessed Redeemer. Today, make a point of showing Him the ultimate respect and reverence both in actions and with the words you speak. Reverence is a gift you can offer Him day after day.

* * *

Lord, I honor You! You're so worthy, Father. May I never be found guilty of disrespecting or dishonoring You. May I always bow the knee to the One who created me and makes all things new in my life. You're worthy to be praised, Lord! Amen.

47

Sentimentality & Tenderness

*Be kind to one another, tenderhearted, forgiving one
another, as God in Christ forgave you.*
EPHESIANS 4:32 ESV

She's one of the sweetest people you've ever met, a true friend.
Her tenderness sets her apart from others. She knows how to
deal gently with people, even those who don't treat her with
as much tenderness in return. Not everyone understands her
heart for the downtrodden, but that doesn't stop her. She's a
true representation of Christ, one who forgives quickly, treats
others with kindness, and is tenderhearted to all. And you want
to be more like her. So you watch closely as she leans in to care
for one in need. You observe her gentle spirit as she brushes
off the insults and pain others attempt to bring. This friend of
yours is more than just a lover of people who goes unnoticed
by the masses. She's a true gift, one given by the Lord to share
His heart with the world.

*Lord, thank You for my tenderhearted friends. I learn so much
from them. May I be just as sentimental, just as tender,
that others will see You in my actions. Amen.*

48

Tribe (Your Inner Circle)

The following day he arrived in Caesarea.
Cornelius was expecting them and had called
together his relatives and close friends.
ACTS 10:24 NIV

Who's in your tribe. . .your inner circle? Pause to think about that for a moment. The people who God has surrounded you with—family members, close friends, caring coworkers—aren't there by accident. Many have been strategically placed in your life to sharpen you, to shape you, to wrap arms of love around you during seasons of distress. Pause to think about the ones who've poured into your life over the past few years. No doubt you'll have quite a list. What a gift these people are. Now think about this in reverse. Whom have you loved? Whom have you sharpened? Who would count you among their tribe members? Remember, it's great to receive love and care from others but even greater to give.

Lord, thank You for those who care enough to pour into my
life. I'm grateful for my tribe. Each person has a role to play.
Now I ask You to show me whom I can help, Father. I want to
be a giver, a lover of people. Lead me to those
who need me most, I pray. Amen.

49

Dessert

Nehemiah said, "Go and enjoy choice food and sweet drinks, and send some to those who have nothing prepared. This day is holy to our Lord. Do not grieve, for the joy of the LORD is your strength."
NEHEMIAH 8:10 NIV

Did you ever pause to think about who came up with the idea of dessert? Wouldn't you love to meet that person and give him a hug? Maybe you've heard the old saying "Desserts is stressed spelled backward." It just makes everything better. Dessert is the icing on your proverbial cake, a reward for a job well done, a special treat on a hard day. It's that little "something extra" to bring a smile to your face. So what are your favorites? Chocolate cake? Ice cream? Cookies? Brownies? Lemon bars?... Why not whip up a batch to bring a smile to the faces of those you love? Then settle in around the table, relax with a cup of coffee, and share some special moments with loved ones.

Lord, I love the sweet life. I enjoy coming up with desserts (even the sugar-free versions). It's the little "something extra" that means so much, Lord. I especially love eating dessert with those I love. It's the perfect ending to a long, hard day. Thanks for giving us such treats, Lord. Amen.

50

Loving God

Jesus replied: " 'Love the Lord your God with all your heart and with all your soul and with all your mind.' "
MATTHEW 22:37 NIV

～

Have you ever considered the notion that the ability to love God is a gift? Think about that for a moment. We claim to love so many things—our possessions, our pets, our homes, our family members. But to love God, whom we've never seen with our eyes or heard with our physical ears? How did we get from point A to point B, from not even knowing Him to loving Him so fully? Perhaps you've heard that old song "To Know Him Is to Love Him." That's how it is with God too. We love Him because we've taken the time to get to know Him. The more we know Him, the more we know we can trust Him. Oh, how our hearts overflow with love for our Daddy-God!

Father, how I love You. You've already proven Your love for me so many times over. Now I'm free to respond to that love with full abandon. I adore You, heavenly Father—with all my heart, all my soul, and all my mind. Thank You for teaching me how to love. Amen.

51

Being Loved by God

But I am like an olive tree flourishing in the house of God;
I trust in God's unfailing love for ever and ever.
PSALM 52:8 NIV

Comfortable. Safe. Welcome. Adored. There's nothing that compares to the love of God. It forgives the unforgivable, adores the unadorable, and rebuilds the shattered, broken heart. It emboldens you, gives you the courage to put one foot in front of the other even on days when you feel you simply can't. Knowing you're loved by the Creator of all is one of the finest gifts you'll ever unwrap. There's nothing you can do to cause God to un-love you. There's no place you can hide where His love won't seek you out. That deep, abiding love penetrates the darkness and wraps you in its embrace often when you least expect or deserve it. How beautiful, the love of God. How precious to know He has our hearts!

I don't deserve Your love, Father, and yet You pour it
over me like oil from a jar. It makes all things bearable,
all things right. I sense it, Lord, and stand in awe that
You would adore this flawed, broken daughter.
How I love You in return, Father. Amen.

Relationships

But Ruth said, "Do not urge me to leave you or to return from following you. For where you go I will go, and where you lodge I will lodge. Your people shall be my people, and your God my God."
RUTH 1:16 ESV

∼

Mother. Father. Daughter. Son. Brother. Sister. Aunt. Uncle. Friend. Coworker. Pastor. God has given you so many people to connect with in this life. He longs for you to "relate" to them, to enter into relationship. Entering isn't always easy, and sustaining can be difficult at times too, but the payoff is significant. Nothing beats a lifelong friend. She knows you from the inside out and loves you anyway. So look closely at those in your inner circle. They're not there by accident. Ask the Lord to show you how you can grow closer to each one to "relate" as best you can. Don't hover. Enter into the depths. These relationships can teach you how to love God more deeply and how to embrace life more fully.

. . . .

Lord, thank You for showing me how to grow my relationships—even the hard ones. I don't want to hang on the fringes, Father. I want to go "all in" with those You've placed in my life. Thank You for showing me how to relate with each one, Father. Amen.

53

Butterfly Kisses

Behold, children are a heritage from the LORD,
the fruit of the womb a reward.
PSALM 127:3 ESV

Children are miraculous gifts from the Lord. We learn to communicate with them before they are even born, holding our hands on Mommy's belly and singing songs of love over them. We coddle and coo when they are born, then plant sweet kisses in their hair as we cradle them in our arms. As they grow, we continue to find new ways to express our love—with hugs, kisses, tickles, and the ultimate. . .the butterfly kiss. If you've never heard of this childlike kiss, it's simple! You "kiss" the little one's cheek with your eyelashes. There's something so precious, so innocent, about sharing butterfly kisses with that little darling. It forms a bond and causes your heart to flutter. . . much like a butterfly!

Father, I love the many ways You show me that You love me.
Thank You for showing me how to love the little ones in my
life too. I want to make lasting memories, Lord, to leave
a legacy. May they always remember the deep,
abiding love I have for them. Amen.

54

The Greatest of These

For now there are faith, hope, and love.
But of these three, the greatest is love.
1 CORINTHIANS 13:13 CEV

God has given us the world. All gifts are at our disposal. He builds our faith, gives us hope in the darkest hour, and loves us in ways we could only imagine before giving our hearts to Him. If you were to stop right now and ask God, "What's the greatest of all the gifts You've given me?" do you know what He would say? Love. Love is the greatest gift. It transcends every other. Love can do what nothing else can—build faith, build hope, build trust, build relationships. Love is the core, the center of the wheel, the part upon which everything else spins. Today, make sure love is at the core of your life. Above your work. Above your money matters. Above your passion to succeed. The greatest of these. . .is love.

Father, may I never forget that love is the key to all things.
If I want to succeed in business, I must learn to love those
I work with/for. If I want to do well in my relationships,
love must lead the way. You gave me the perfect
formula, Lord, when You told me to put love first.
That's what I choose to do today, Father. Amen.

55

Parents-in-Love

" 'Honor your father and your mother, as the LORD your God
commanded you, that your days may be long, and that
it may go well with you in the land that the
LORD your God is giving you.' "

DEUTERONOMY 5:16 ESV

Many don't grow up with biological parents. And others don't have parental figures at all. Some have parents who didn't leave a very good legacy. Some folks reach adulthood and then develop friendships with older, more mature people who fulfill a parental role. (You could call these folks "parents-in-love.") These amazing people fill the gap for all you missed while growing up. They mentor. They love. They teach. They advise. They care. Simply put, they adore you as one would adore a child. So who are these parents-in-love in your life? Pause to think through the ones who've poured into your life. A neighbor, perhaps? An older friend from church? A coworker? If you look close, you'll probably see that God has surrounded you with parents-in-love who adore you and are happy to be a part of the family.

Father, thank You for the parents-in-love You've placed in my life. I've learned so much from them. May I return the favor by mentoring young people who need my love as well. Amen.

Communication with the Father

*Call to me and I will answer you, and will tell you great
and hidden things that you have not known.*
JEREMIAH 33:3 ESV

Imagine what your life would have been like if your father
had refused to speak to you. What if he'd booted you from
his presence, unwilling to hear your stories or dry your tears?
Perhaps your childhood was a bit like that. You didn't know or
couldn't communicate with your earthly father. How precious,
then, the knowledge that your heavenly Father extends His
arms, ready to spend quality time with You. He wants to listen
to your heart's cry, but He also has a few things to whisper into
your ear as well. This communication is such a blessing, isn't
it? It shows us just how much He cares. And God doesn't just
want to hear how you spent your day. He longs for you to pour
out your deepest cares and concerns so that He can kiss away
every tear and bandage the broken places. What a precious and
loving Father and how wonderful His heart for us!

*Daddy-God, You have always been so welcoming. You've
encouraged me to share my news, good and bad, so that You
can minister to my heart. Today I lean in close, Father,
that I might hear those precious words of love You're
whispering in my ear. Oh, how I praise You! Amen.*

57

Purity

*Don't let anyone look down on you because you are young,
but set an example for the believers in speech,
in conduct, in love, in faith and in purity.*
1 TIMOTHY 4:12 NIV

White as snow. Untouched. Pristine. The word *purity* brings
these images to mind. Perhaps you hear this word and shudder.
You've been through so much. You feel dirty. Used. Broken. God
can take you just as you are and restore every area of your life,
including your purity. He longs to do just that. Don't be afraid
to approach Him, to be vulnerable, to admit the areas of your
life where you've been weak. He's not shocked by the news of
where you've been. He was right there, loving you even then.
Ask Him to restore you; then watch in wonder as He does just
that. He adores you, after all. You're His daughter, His child,
His beloved. When He looks at you through the sacrifice of His
Son, He sees an innocent child in need of her Daddy-God's love.

*Father, thank You for restoring my purity. You're an
amazing Daddy, only seeing the good in me.
How I love You, Lord. Thank You for the work
You're doing in my heart and life. Amen.*

58

Patience

The end of a matter is better than its beginning,
and patience is better than pride.
ECCLESIASTES 7:8 NIV

$\sim$

"Patience is a virtue." You've likely heard this phrase a time or two, probably while you were waiting for something to happen. And while it is a virtue, a positive trait, it's also a gift, for most of the learning comes during the waiting. Think about it. If a mother didn't have to patiently wait nine months for a baby to be born, would she discover all the nuances of pregnancy? If the delivery happened in minutes instead of hours, would she appreciate the sacrifice of giving herself for the birth of the child? If she didn't have to wait to watch that baby crawl, walk, and then run, would she appreciate each milestone? She waits not because it's the right thing to do but because waiting itself is a gift. To wait with patience? Priceless.

Lord, I get it. You're not "trying" my patience. You're offering
me the gift of patience. Like a mother who's expecting,
I'm wide open to learn the lessons You're teaching, Father.
I know there are many I have yet to learn. Thank You for
Your diligence in my life. I wait with expectation. Amen.

A Beating Heart

Keep your heart with all vigilance,
for from it flow the springs of life.
PROVERBS 4:23 ESV

Its pitter-pat keeps us going day to day, hour to hour, minute to minute. And yet we're scarcely aware of its presence. The human heart beats approximately one hundred thousand times a day. It sends two thousand gallons of blood coursing through your body. It has the task of keeping you alive. What a miraculous gift! Today, pause for a moment and pay attention to your heartbeat by pressing your finger to your wrist. Feel that pulse? It's a reminder that you are here for a reason. You're alive on Planet Earth "for such a time as this," for a reason. You'll never doubt your purpose again as long as you feel your heart beating within you.

Lord, I'm grateful for the reminder that my beating heart is
a sign You have great things ahead for me. That amazing,
life-giving wonder is more than just a human organ; it's a sign
that I have a purpose. Thank You for that reminder, Father.
I won't take these moments for granted. Amen.

60

Springtime

For behold, the winter is past; the rain is over and gone.
The flowers appear on the earth, the time of singing has
come, and the voice of the turtledove is heard in our land.
SONG OF SOLOMON 2:11–12 ESV

Can you see the tiny buds breaking through the hard clay? Can you sense the majesty in new life as flowers burst into bloom? This joyous season is a representation of all that's good in this world as dead things spring to life once more. It's a season of picnics and kite flying, flower blossoms and breaks from school. More than anything, it's the perfect time to reflect on the goodness of God as He regenerates life all around us. Spring brings with it hope just as each new bud brings hope of a soon-coming blossom. What was once dead, dormant, is now fully alive. Oh praise Him! What a wonderful reminder that our cold, weary hearts can spring to life anew as well.

Lord, today I offer You my heart. It's still beating, Father,
but I don't always feel fully alive. Sometimes I'm just going
through the motions. Today, I ask You to breathe the gift
of springtime into my heart that I might spring to
life—in all of its fullness—once more. Amen.

Spring Break

Ask rain from the LORD in the season of the spring
rain, from the LORD who makes the storm clouds,
and he will give them showers of rain,
to everyone the vegetation in the field.
ZECHARIAH 10:1 ESV

What do you think of when you hear the words *Take a break!*?
Do you see yourself in the recliner, feet elevated? Maybe you
picture yourself at the beach, basking in the warmth of the afternoon sun. Perhaps you envision yourself sitting quietly on the
porch swing, drinking in the cool morning air. No matter how
you view the word *break*, be it siesta or vacation, God is keen
on you taking one. He never intended for you to keep going,
going, going until you've worn yourself out. So give yourself a
break this spring. Step away from your projects for a few hours
(or even a few days), and enjoy the changing season. Observe
the flowers as they burst forth in glorious display. Give those
gorgeous blue skies more than just a passing glance. Look for
pictures in the clouds. Just. . .be. And in the process, discover
peace, joy, and fulfillment.

Thank You for spring break, Lord, even if it's short-lived.
I'm grateful for the reminder that it's healthy to step away
from my workload and spend quality time in Your
presence. Today I choose to do just that. Amen.

62

Song in the Heart

The LORD is my strength and my shield; my heart trusts
in him, and he helps me. My heart leaps for joy,
and with my song I praise him.
PSALM 28:7 NIV

∿

Bubbling up from your innermost being, its melody and lyrics compel you to sing. That song in your heart transports you, lifts you above your problems, and energizes you to face difficult situations head-on. You didn't plant it there. It arose from a deep, abiding relationship with the Giver of the song, God Himself. When you enter into relationship with the Lord, He places a new song in your heart. Your spirit is born again, and your lips long to sing out praise for all the magnificent changes taking place in your heart. What a gift, this life-song! It's a reminder of all the Lord has done. So go ahead! Praise Him with a song!

* * *

Lord, I lift my voice in song to You today. It's bubbling up
to the surface, and I can't hold back. When You brought me
back to life, Father, You instantly gave me a new song to
sing. Today I choose to sing it in praise to You. Amen.

A Beautifully Decorated Room

*"A tree from the forest is cut down and worked with an axe
by the hands of a craftsman. They decorate it with silver
and gold; they fasten it with hammer and
nails so that it cannot move."*
JEREMIAH 10:3–4 ESV

It's so much fun to dress up a room. A fresh coat of paint. Pictures on the wall. Wood trim. Just the right mirror. When you transform a room, you're saying, "It's time for a fresh start." Out with the old, in with the new. And walking into that transformed room is good for the heart. Suddenly everything feels fresh, new. It puts you in a more hopeful state of mind. It stirs you to action and makes you want to keep everything tidy. Transformation has that kind of power both in rooms and in our thought life. When we transform our thinking as one would transform a room, we're filled with hope. We want to keep our thoughts tidy and clean. We are filled with new possibilities. So what's keeping you? Choose a room in your home and get busy. Transform!

*I love to decorate, Lord. It's fun to shuffle furniture around,
change the color of the walls, and hang new curtains.
I'm always so excited when the work is done because I feel
like I've accomplished something fun. Thanks for the
reminder that You long to transform my thoughts just
as I've transformed rooms. I open myself
to the possibilities, Lord! Amen.*

64

Happy Thoughts

Set your minds on things above, not on earthly things.
COLOSSIANS 3:2 NIV

You can't seem to help yourself. Your thoughts keep drifting back to that one thing you really don't need to be focused on. That mistake you made. That problem you can't fix. That person who annoys you. Oh, you try to shift gears, but minutes later your thoughts have reverted to that dark spot once again. If only you could somehow redirect your thinking. Oh, but you can! In fact, as a child of God, you can call on the One who created you to set your mind on things above, not on earthly things. God can take your darkest thoughts, your deepest painful memory, and add light, levity, clarity. He can refocus your thought-life and help you adjust to a whole new way of thinking. This ability to reset your thoughts is a gift! God knows you're ready for a shift in your thinking, and He's right there, ready to walk you through the process.

Lord, thank You for the reminder that I don't have to be stuck. My mind can be free. I don't have to dwell on negative or bad things any longer. I can set my mind on things above, Father, and You will transform my thinking. Thank You in advance, Lord! Amen.

65

Miracles

God did extraordinary miracles through Paul.
ACTS 19:11 NIV

A baby's first cry. Amazing news from the doctor after a lengthy illness. Protection from a car accident. Miracles come when you least expect them, when you're hanging on by a thread, wondering if things can possibly work out. They are evidence of God's hand at work, doing the impossible. What are you believing in God for today? A financial miracle? A miracle in your health, your family, your home? The Lord is still in the miracle-working business today, so open yourself to the possibilities. Begin to anticipate the supernatural intervention of God. He can turn even the darkest situation into a shining illustration of His love and mercy.

Lord, Your hand is at work in every area of my life.
I've watched You perform miracles in my relationships.
You've mended fences over and over again. I've witnessed
financial miracles and have seen loved ones rise up from
their sickbeds completely whole. What a generous and
loving Father You are. You care enough to intervene
on our behalf. How I praise You, Lord. Amen.

66

Your Job

Whatever you do, work heartily,
as for the Lord and not for men.
COLOSSIANS 3:23 ESV

It's more than just a place you go to work or a way to earn a paycheck. Your job is a gift, filled with endless possibilities. The people you've learned to love, the desk covered with papers, the emails, phone calls, and so on. . .they're all opportunities to communicate with people you wouldn't have met otherwise. Your job is, in essence, your chance to touch the world and to share the love of Jesus with others. And you love the opportunity. You seize each day as if it might be your last, spreading laughter and joy to all you come in contact with. You're a conduit of God's grace and love, someone others enjoy being around. How precious this workplace!

I'm so grateful for my job, Lord. I'm happy to have the
income, of course, but I'm also blessed beyond measure
that You've given me new friendships and the opportunity
to spread Your love to others. May I be the best
possible representation of You, Father. Amen.

Honorable Intentions

*Do not lie to one another, seeing that you have
put off the old self with its practices.*
COLOSSIANS 3:9 ESV

Have you ever taken the time to check your intentions? Do you know why you do the things you do? What propels you? Intentions are a powerful thing. They motivate us, drive us forward, give us energy. But not all intentions are good, are they? Some folks are propelled by evil intentions. They're pushed to the limits because of anger, fear, or revenge. Not so with the believer, however! God longs for His girls to be women of integrity, motivated by good not evil. As a child of the King, your intentions should be pure and honest, a gift you offer others. Today, take inventory. Do an "intention check." Ask God to reveal anything that's pushing you in the wrong direction. Check and double-check your heart, for it will be your guide.

*Lord, I'll admit my intentions aren't always good.
Sometimes I do "good works" with wrong intentions—to get
a pat on the back or applause. Today I ask You to reveal any
impure intentions. I want to turn things around in a hurry,
Father, so let's get busy on this heart check! Amen.*

68

Five Senses

Every good gift and every perfect gift is from above,
coming down from the Father of lights, with whom
there is no variation or shadow due to change.
JAMES 1:17 ESV

Senses. Can you imagine life without them? To not hear the sound of a baby's cry? To never smell the aroma of popcorn filling the air? To never see a golden sunset or a puppy at play? To never feel the sand under your feet or taste the sweetness of a cupcake? How often we forget that our senses are a gift from our creative heavenly Father, who longs for us to experience life to its fullest. Which of the five senses are you most grateful for? Which would be the hardest to give up? As you think this through, remember to praise God for offering His kiddos all the sights, sounds, smells, tastes, and touches that this great big world has to offer.

Lord, I'm so grateful for my senses. How dull life would be
without them! You're so creative, Father, to give us the gifts
of sight, smell, touch, sound, and taste. You want Your kids
to experience life to the fullest, and that's just what
I plan to do. Praise You, Father. Amen!

69

Music

The trumpeters and musicians joined in unison to give praise and thanks to the LORD. Accompanied by trumpets, cymbals and other instruments, the singers raised their voices in praise to the LORD and sang: "He is good; his love endures forever." Then the temple of the LORD was filled with the cloud.
2 CHRONICLES 5:13 NIV

Ah, music! Where would we be without it? Loaded with crescendos and beautifully paced phrases that allow us to catch our breath, it provides a sound track for our day-to-day living. It lifts our spirits and calms us when we need calming. Music is a joyous expression of everything we are, everything we believe, and all we hope to become. It draws us closer to God and reminds us that heaven will resound with songs of praise, with melodies yet unheard by the human ear! Here on earth we rehearse with hymns and worship songs beautifully crafted by skilled artisans. Aren't you grateful for the composers among us? The ability to compose a melody and then add harmonies is truly God-given. What a gift they share with us!

Lord, I lift a song of praise to You today.
Thank You for the skilled musicians who point
humankind toward You. Bless them, I pray. Amen.

70

Satisfaction

*"Blessed are those who hunger and thirst for
righteousness, for they shall be satisfied."*
MATTHEW 5:6 ESV

Have you ever considered the fact that satisfaction is a gift?
That wonderful feeling you have after a good meal, that
comfortable sensation that you've done right by someone,
that overwhelming feeling of blessing as you observe your
home and other provisions. . .all are various ways of feeling
satisfied. How rough life must be for those who never feel a
sense of satisfaction. How exhausting to always long for more,
to feel cheated, to dream of bigger, better, greater, instead of
appreciating what's right in front of you. Oh, but you're not
like that! You are blessed by the best and completely at peace
with all He's done for you. Why not thank the Lord for all He's
done in your life?

*I'm grateful, Father! You've met every need and satisfied
me at every turn even when I didn't deserve it. I want to
experience gratitude to the fullest, so I plan to stick
close to You. May I never grow dissatisfied
or turn from You, Lord. Amen.*

Personal Contentment

*But I have calmed and quieted myself, I am like a weaned
child with its mother; like a weaned child I am content.*
PSALM 131:2 NIV

How often have you said, "I'm okay being me. I wouldn't swap
lives with anyone else." Contentment is a great thing, especially
when it comes to who you are as a person and as a child of
God. Far too many people wrestle with discontentment over
how they look, where they live, what they own (or don't own),
and whether or not their dreams will come true. Learning to be
content in whatever state you're in (physically or emotionally) is
so important. When you really grab hold of contentment, when
you start to understand that God created you a certain height,
hair color, personality type, and so on, you can settle in and
begin to enjoy being yourself. (And hey, there's only one you!)
Today, look at contentment as a gift, one you have to accept.
Extend those hands and grab on to it. Let it take you to a place
where you can love yourself as Christ loves you.

*Lord, I haven't always loved myself. I see so many flaws when
I look in the mirror or when I compare myself and my life
with others. Thank You for the reminder that I'm created
by You and can learn to love myself fully. I know that
contentment will follow, Father, and I'm grateful. Amen.*

A Home to Clean

By knowledge the rooms are filled with all
precious and pleasant riches.
PROVERBS 24:4 ESV

Smelly tennis shoes in the hallway. Dirty socks strewn across a teenager's bedroom floor. Dog hair on the sofa. Crusty dishes piled in the kitchen sink. These are the daily visuals we face in the average home. We strive for perfection but fall short, especially on days when we have to rush the kids to soccer practice or buzz out the front door to get to that PTA meeting. Life is crazy-busy, but home is where the heart is. That special place where you gather with those you love, it's one of the finest gifts you've ever received. Sure, the baseboards need a coat of paint, and yes, the windows need to be washed; but your home is truly a sanctuary from the world outside—a sometimes messy, always chaotic sanctuary. Settle in and enjoy it!

Father, I'm so grateful for my home, even on the messy days.
You've given my family a place of shelter from the storms
of life, a sanctuary from the chaos of this world (though we
do create a bit of chaos ourselves). I want to keep it in
good shape, but even when things are a bit out of place,
I will celebrate this fabulous gift You've given me. Amen.

73

Laundry

"And why do you worry about clothes? See how the flowers of the field grow. They do not labor or spin."
MATTHEW 6:28 NIV

Perhaps you're surrounded by piles of it. Piles and piles, in fact. Shirts. Pants. Skirts. Blouses. Unmentionables. Towels. Washcloths. Socks. Lots and lots of socks. You sort by color and toss items into the washer then forget to put them into the dryer. . . so you start the washer again. Or maybe you toss the items into the dryer and leave them for days. Such are the woes of laundry. Oh, but what a blessing to have clothes to wash! May we never take for granted the fact that God has provided for our every need right down to the clothes we wear. Whether they're clean or not, praise God for those jeans, that T-shirt, that cute dress. He has you covered. . .literally!

Lord, I don't recall the last time I actually thanked You for my laundry, but I'm starting to see what a blessing it is. Sure, it's a lot of work, but laundry is a visible reminder that You care enough to meet my needs. You provide covering, and all because of Your great love for me. I'm so grateful, Father. Amen.

74

Shoes

And God is able to make all grace abound to you,
so that having all sufficiency in all things at all
times, you may abound in every good work.
2 CORINTHIANS 9:8 ESV

Millions of feet across the globe have grown calloused from walking barefoot. People get accustomed to the pain. After a while they barely notice it. The rest of the world grumbles if a shoe rubs a little blister or causes discomfort. They can't fathom how different their lives would be if they had been born in another part of the world. It's nearly impossible to fathom how complicated life would be if you had to go without shoes. Your closet is filled with them, after all, and in so many different styles and colors. Tennis shoes. Boots. Heels. Sandals. You can pick and choose, depending on your clothing of the day. Winter shoes, summer shoes. . .you have your choice of so many. Today, as you ponder the shoe situation around the world, why not do a little research online and see how you can "shod the feet" of a child in a third-world country. Now there's a comfortable idea!

Lord, thank You for the reminder that people need my help.
I want to do something, Lord. Show me how I can play a role
in providing the gift of shoes to those who need them. Amen.

Positive Influences

Do not be deceived: "Bad company ruins good morals."
1 CORINTHIANS 15:33 ESV

They point you in the right direction. Their positive, upbeat actions and reactions encourage you to better yourself. They face the same choices all friends face, but they usually go with the better of the two. These positive influences in your life have guided you from early childhood until now. God has surrounded you with them, in fact. That little girl who refused to cheat on her spelling test? That teenage friend who refused to cross the line with her boyfriend? That college roommate who wasn't into the all-night partying thing? These fine people were gifts placed by God to help you along life's journey. And He's called you to be a positive influence in someone's life as well. Look for opportunities to do that as you head out on your way today. Whose eyes are watching you? What sort of influence will you be?

Lord, thank You for the many, many people You've placed in my life to influence me and point me toward You. Every teacher, family member, or friend who played a role was strategically placed. I'm so grateful for every single one, Father. Amen.

76

Encouragement

Therefore encourage one another and build one another up, just as you are doing.
1 THESSALONIANS 5:11 ESV

It's fun to look at the prefix of a word. To "en"-courage someone means you're ready to bolster their courage, making them stronger, bolder, healthier. Think of how the meaning would shift if you changed the prefix to "dis-" instead of "en-." What a bummer! Aren't you grateful for the encouragers in your life today? What a gift they are. Those little pats on the back, those "atta-girls" are often just what you need to keep going. God is so good to surround us with "en-" friends. So which kind of friend are you? Make up your mind to "en-" someone today. And don't forget to pray for the ones who lift you up.

Lord, I hardly know where to begin. You've placed so many encouragers in my life over the years—teachers, parents, friends, coworkers, and so on. Please bless them, Father. Encourage their hearts. And while we're at it, I want to ask You to use me as an encourager too. Give me words to speak the next time I come in contact with a friend who's discouraged. Speak through me, I pray. Amen.

Comfort

Blessed are those who mourn,
for they will be comforted.
MATTHEW 5:4 NIV

Warm, fuzzy slippers. A cozy blanket. Hot chicken soup when you have the sniffles. All of these things bring comfort—that feeling of contentment or peace that settles over you and convinces you that all is well. No doubt you've loved the feeling since infancy, when your parents swaddled you in that tiny baby blanket. You enjoyed it as you grew, as your mama fed you chicken and dumplings or your favorite dessert—warm brownies with ice cream. Perhaps you experienced it as a young wife, cradled in your husband's comforting embrace. That feeling you get when you feel relaxed, safe, secure is a gift from heaven. Comfort is God's way of swaddling you and putting tiny kisses on your forehead. It's His special way of saying, "Rest easy. Everything's going to be all right." Praise Him for the comfort that only He can bring!

Lord, I'm so grateful for the gift of comfort. You've intervened
in my life so many times, comforting me when no one else
could. I've heard Your still, small voice as You've whispered,
"Peace, be still," to my heart. No one can
comfort as You can, Father. Amen.

Forgiveness

*"Therefore, my friends, I want you to know that through
Jesus the forgiveness of sins is proclaimed to you."*
ACTS 13:38 NIV

A clean slate. A washing away of every stain. A solid word from
the Lord: "I have this one covered. It's behind you now." That's
what forgiveness offers, a chance to begin again, fresh and new,
no lingering blots from yesterday's sin. But forgiveness isn't
just something you receive. It's a gift you offer—to the one who
wounded you with her words, to the friend who left you out, to
the child who disrespected you. It's an opportunity to release
the pain of yesterday by blotting out acts against you, whether
deliberate or unintentional. Forgiving others isn't easy, nor does
it seem fair at times. But it's the finest gift you can give yourself, for when you release it to others, the benefits to your own
heart and mind are substantial. Talk about a boomerang effect!

*Lord, I don't always feel like forgiving others,
but I definitely see the benefit of it. And how can I hold
others in unforgiveness when You've blotted out my
sins? Today, help me to release the angst, the pain,
the heartache. Show me how to forgive that
I might walk in total healing. Amen.*

79

Kindness of Strangers

David asked, "Is there anyone still left of the house of Saul to whom I can show kindness for Jonathan's sake?"
2 SAMUEL 9:1 NIV

Have you ever found yourself in a situation where you had to rely on the kindness of strangers? Perhaps your car broke down on the side of the highway, or you caused a minor fender bender. You had to rely on someone who stopped to lend a hand. Maybe your child got sick, and you had no way to call your spouse, so you borrowed someone else's phone. Perhaps you found yourself in the grocery store with no debit card and watched in amazement as someone else paid for your groceries. In those moments when we really need someone at our side, it's very often someone we've never met before. God bless those Good Samaritans for sticking with us and showing us the kindness of the Lord.

Father, there are angels all around me! I know because I've watched them at work. They've appeared from out of the blue in my moments of need. It's humbling to let a total stranger intervene on my behalf, but I'm so grateful You have me covered, Lord. Thank You (and them). Amen.

80

Respect

Show proper respect to everyone, love the family
of believers, fear God, honor the emperor.
1 PETER 2:17 NIV

There's an old adage that respect has to be earned. To respect or admire someone is a gift you offer them, usually based on how they've treated you. The Bible gives us a slightly different slant on the word. Believers are called to respect those in authority over them even if the actions of the individual don't seem to warrant it. Perhaps you've struggled to respect someone in your life—a parent who mistreated you, a teacher who embarrassed you, a friend who stabbed you in the back. How are we to show respect to these and the many others who've hurt us? In many cases, respecting the position is the best we can do. We do our best to speak kindly of this person simply because it honors God to treat others as we want to be treated.

Lord, I'll admit I don't always respect those in authority
over me. Sometimes their actions lead me to other feelings.
Today I choose to forgive. Show me how to respect the
position even if I'm unable to respect the person. Amen.

84

Created in God's Image

God created man in His own image, in the image of God
He created him; male and female He created them.
GENESIS 1:27 NASB

Our very creative God could have chosen to form us in any image. (He did create some pretty unique animals, after all.) But He made a purposeful decision to create man in His image. Wow. The next time you look in the mirror, instead of fussing and fretting over the wrinkles, freckles, and such, instead of wondering why you have your mother's wide hips or your grandpa's knobby knees, why not ponder the truth: you are created in the image of Almighty God. That far exceeds any physical traits you might have inherited from your ancestors. And while you are completely unique in appearance from all others on the planet, you carry inside of you the DNA of the Creator of the universe. Now that's a gift worth celebrating!

Lord, I'm created in Your image! I'm made to look, act,
and live like You. It's part of my DNA. Today I ask that You
stir up all of the good things I've inherited from You and
help me to live to my fullest potential so that all will see
You in me. I want to be a reflection of You. Amen.

Holiness

"Who is like You among the gods, O LORD? Who is like You, majestic in holiness, awesome in praises, working wonders?"
EXODUS 15:11 NASB

If you were raised in a legalistic home—each day filled with excessive do's and don'ts—you might see holiness as something you strive for but never quite attain. Perhaps you spent your younger years wondering if you would ever live up to the expectations placed on you by parents or church leaders. Maybe you stopped trying, drawing the conclusion that holiness was impossible. There's good news! You never had to "try" to be holy. Holiness was never meant to be carried on your shoulders. When you give your heart to the Lord, when you enter into relationship with Him through His Son, the holiness and purity of Christ washes away every stain and purifies you. You take on His holiness. This redemptive process is an amazing gift. So rest easy. Sure, God wants you to do your best, but if you mess up—and we all do—He's right there, ready to help you begin again.

I'm so glad it's not all on me, Lord. I'm tired of trying to behave and live within such tight confines. What a relief to know that my salvation, my cleansing, doesn't come as a result of my actions. Jesus took care of all that for me on the cross. I accept that cleansing today, Father, and praise You for it. Amen.

83

Redemption

*Christ redeemed us from the curse of the law by
becoming a curse for us, for it is written:
"Cursed is everyone who is hung on a pole."*
GALATIANS 3:13 NIV

～⤳～

Remember those little stamp booklets your mother or grandmother kept? She filled the squares with stamps then redeemed the book at the grocery store, the gas station, or any other redemption center. That little book was worth something but only if you cashed it in. That's what our life in Christ is like too. We're redeemed. Purchased by the blood of the Lamb. When Jesus died on the cross, the "cashing in" process took place. Talk about value! Oh, how we praise the Lord for the gift of redemption. While we were yet sinners, unable to save ourselves, He swept in and rescued us, even going so far as to take our place. What an amazing gift redemption is!

. . . .

*Thank You, Lord, for the act of redemption! While I was yet a
sinner, separated from You, You swept in and redeemed me.
Where there was nothing good or valuable in me, You brought
value. I've been purchased by Your Son, though I never
did a thing to deserve it. What a gift, Father!
What an amazing gift. Amen.*

84

Light

The light shines in the darkness,
and the darkness has not overcome it.
JOHN 1:5 ESV

✦

Remember as a child how you used to blindfold one another and try to find your way around in the darkness? Without the light to guide you, knees got skinned, elbows bumped, and toes stubbed. We depend on light to offer direction and safety to our environment. The same is true on a spiritual level. Without the light of God's love, His vision, His wisdom, we would stagger with no sense of purpose. When was the last time you asked the Lord to shine His light on a situation in your life? It's time to flip the switch and shed light on that situation. He wants to guide you through it, but that can only happen if you submit to the process. No more staggering around in the dark for you. Pull off that blindfold, and walk boldly into the light.

* * *

I'm tired of wandering in the dark, Father. I feel lost so much
of the time. I don't know which way to turn, which opportunity
to grab hold of. Today I ask You to shine Your light on the
situations I'm facing so that I can have clear direction.
Hold tightly to my hand and lead me, Lord.
I want to walk in the safety of Your light. Amen.

85

Generosity

*"In all things I have shown you that by working hard
in this way we must help the weak and remember the words
of the Lord Jesus, how he himself said, 'It is more
blessed to give than to receive.'"*
ACTS 20:35 ESV

Generous people are such a gift! They go out of their way to
surprise and delight others, and usually when folks least suspect
it. Their sacrificial giving is done with a smile on their face and
a song in their heart. How is such generosity possible for the
believer? Does it come naturally? It should! We are created with
God's DNA, and He's a very generous friend. So go ahead—pay
for the meal of the person behind you in line at the coffee shop.
Send a bouquet of flowers to a friend in need. Pick up the tab
when you're out with a young couple. Leave groceries on the
front porch of an elderly neighbor's home. Extend the hand of
generosity—the gift that keeps on giving.

*Lord, I want others to see me as a generous person. May it never
be said of me that I behaved in a stingy or self-focused way.
I want to lavish Your love, Your joy, and Your hope to all I meet.
Show me whom I can bless today, Father, then give me creative
ideas that I might leave Your mark on their hearts. Amen.*

86

Organization

For God is not a God of confusion but of peace.
1 CORINTHIANS 14:33 ESV

❧

A clean desktop. A tidy drawer. A colorful shelf filled with carefully folded clothes. A sink emptied of its dishes. A garage with everything in its place. These are either pipe dreams or how you live. . .and you get to choose. Few things are more satisfying than an organized work or living space. Clutter causes chaos and confusion and wastes precious time, but a tidy area can bring peace. Some people have the gift of organization. If you're not one of them, swap tasks with a friend. Offer to prepare a meal or bake a cake in exchange for her help. Chances are she's probably already chomping at the bit to help anyway. Go ahead. . .let her share that gift of organization with you. It'll be a win-win situation.

* *

Lord, I want so desperately to be organized, but it's not always easy. Sometimes my life is just a jumble of clutter. Show me how to bring order to the spaces You've entrusted to me, Father. Send someone to help. I want to keep things tidy, not just to reduce my stress level, but to honor You. Amen.

Long Phone Calls

Love one another with brotherly affection.
Outdo one another in showing honor.
ROMANS 12:10 ESV

Remember what life was like before cell phones and text messages? Before the days of social media, folks would pick up the telephone and make a call to a friend or loved one. Teenage girls lounged for hours on Saturday afternoons, gabbing with friends. Mothers and fathers took much-anticipated long-distance calls from family members in other states. People couldn't wait to hear from loved ones far away. Sadly, phone calls aren't as common as they once were. Why call when you can shoot off a text in an instant? That's the mentality most folks have. But some of the people in your circle still have the gift of gab and would probably enjoy speaking with you. Today make a decision to call someone you love. Sit for a while. Give her the time she needs to share the latest goings-on in her life. In doing so, you'll be offering a gift that dates back to the olden days.

Thanks for the reminder that phone calls can be fun, Lord.
I'm so busy these days that I don't often call people,
but I want to get back in the habit. Show me
how and where to start, Father. Amen.

88

Freedom to Believe

For freedom Christ has set us free; stand firm therefore,
and do not submit again to a yoke of slavery.
GALATIANS 5:1 ESV

The freedom to believe in God, to worship Him publicly, is a gift—one we can't overlook. Around the globe, believers risk their very lives to follow Christ. They hide away to worship, praying they won't get caught. Many make the ultimate sacrifice, choosing Christ in the face of being ostracized from family members. Some realize their faith, if discovered, will result in death. What a sobering reality. May we never take for granted that which others do not have. May we not see our faith as something that fits so comfortably into society that it doesn't set us apart from the masses. May this freedom never be in vain.

Father, my heart is so heavy for those many, many believers
across the globe who don't have the freedom to worship
You publicly. They hide away in home churches, in secret
places, just to worship, to pray, to read Your Word.
They are willing to risk it all for You, Lord. In comparison,
my faith seems so weak. Bolster me, I pray. Give me a
tenacious faith. Please don't ever let my freedom
become commonplace, Lord. Amen.

Acts of Affection

For this very reason, make every effort to supplement your
faith with virtue, and virtue with knowledge. . .
and godliness with brotherly affection,
and brotherly affection with love.
2 PETER 1:5, 7 ESV

What a rush-about world we live in. People are so busy buzzing from place to place, they don't often notice when others are hurting. How precious to pause long enough to notice. And greater still to offer a shoulder, a hand, a prayer, a sweet word of affection and caring. Nothing ministers to a hurting person more than the gentle touch of someone who understands. So be that someone. Today, ask the Lord to open your eyes to those around you. . .to *really* open your eyes. To see the one who's walking through a divorce. To minister to the one who's in physical pain. To offer comfort to one who is grieving. Your small act of kindness—a gentle hug, a whispered prayer—could lift that person's spirits and shift her focus. Will you deliver the gift of affection today?

Lord, thank You for the reminder that I can minister to those
in need. I ask that You open my eyes, Father, that I might see
people the way You do. For those who are hurting, give me
words of comfort and compassion, I pray. Amen.

90

Children of the Light

For you were once darkness, but now you are
light in the Lord. Live as children of light.
EPHESIANS 5:8 NIV

∽

You are a child of the light. Let that sink in a moment. You were never meant to walk in darkness. God delivered you from that. When you feel the tug to return to your old habits, old ways of doing things, look that temptation in the face and say, "No thanks! I was never meant for that life. I'm a child of the light." When you choose to stay in the light (as He is in the light), you're leading by example. Others will see your bravery and follow suit. So square those shoulders. You're not a child of the shadows, the darkness. There's plenty of light ahead, and you plan to walk in it every step of the way.

Father, I'm so glad I'm a child of the light. Keep me walking,
eyes fully open toward You. No shifting shadows on my
journey, Lord! These eyes are fixed on You,
fixed on the Light of lights. Amen.

91

Taste Buds

Taste and see that the LORD is good;
blessed is the one who takes refuge in him.
PSALM 34:8 NIV

Salty popcorn. Iced sugar cookies. Crunchy, spicy tacos. Crispy french fries. Creamy banana pudding. These are just a few of the reasons we enjoy having the gift of taste. Have you ever considered how bland life would be if those taste buds were taken away? You could no longer enjoy garlic-infused breadsticks, silky chocolate pie with meringue topping, or (gasp!) that first cup of coffee each morning. Taste buds aren't visible to the human eye, but they play a mighty role in our lives. Sure, we could still consume food without them, but the pleasure would disappear. To remove the gift of taste would be a tragedy! Today, as you're taking a bite of that cheeseburger or nibbling on potato chips, remember to thank our very creative God for giving us the gift of taste. Then take the time to truly enjoy every morsel of food, savoring each delicious bite.

Lord, I'm so grateful for my taste buds. How bland life would be without them! You are such a creative Father, giving Your kids so many fun ways to experience life. Thank You for creating the sense of taste. It's one of my favorites. Amen.

92

Laughter

He will yet fill your mouth with laughter
and your lips with shouts of joy.
JOB 8:21 NIV

Oh, the gift of laughter! How we love that joyous release! It bubbles up inside us and spills over like a fizzy drink exploding all over the room. Once started, it's hard to stop. Then again, why would you want to? Laughter can turn an otherwise bad day into one of hope, peace, and love. Best of all, it's a gift we can share for free. It doesn't cost a cent to lift a friend's spirits by laughing at her joke or giggling at the antics of her toddler. So go ahead. Give yourself permission to have a little fun. Crack a joke or two. Pass along the humor to a loved one or coworker. You know you want to!

I love the gift of laughter, Lord. It comes straight from You.
It provides a much-needed release from the tensions
of the day. Best of all, it's contagious. I can catch it
from my friends. Thank You for giving me so
much to smile and laugh about, Father. Amen.

93

Puppies

She said, "Yes, Lord, yet even the dogs eat the
crumbs that fall from their masters' table."
MATTHEW 15:27 ESV

They wriggle. They nibble. They piddle. They chew your toes and eat your shoes. They leave holes in your blankets and fill holes in your heart. Puppies are one of the finest gifts one can receive. Whether you've adopted a teeny-tiny Chihuahua or a massive Great Dane, a curly poodle or a shaggy cocker spaniel, the puppy stage is a blast (if you can get past the chewing stage, anyway!). There's something magical about cuddling that warm, wiggly pup and feeling her nuzzle against your neck as she settles down for a nap. All of life's cares disappear as you run your hand over that soft fur and plant a tiny kiss on the top of her head. She's yours. You're hers. And all is right with the world.

Oh, how I love puppies, Lord! I could spend hours looking
at pictures of those feisty babies at play. They bring out the
playful side in me and remind me that life is meant to
be fun. Thank You for creating dogs for our comfort
and enjoyment, Father. May we do the best
possible job caring for them in return. Amen.

94

Art

*He has filled them with skill to do every sort of work done by
an engraver or by a designer or by an embroiderer in blue
and purple and scarlet yarns and fine twined linen, or by
a weaver—by any sort of workman or skilled designer.*
EXODUS 35:35 ESV

Paintings on a cathedral ceiling. A child's drawing on a scrap
of paper. A lovely portrait of a family member. A majestic
steeple rising from a simple church building. The design of
a city building, one carefully thought out. Art takes on many
forms. It greets us in the morning as we look at the car we drive
(what a work of art!) and touches us at every turn as we drive
from one place in the city to another. We notice it in company
logos, a friend's doodling, and even on our stationery. Where
would this world be without art and (better yet) artists? Today,
as you take the time to look around you, thank God for inspiring
so many creative people who've developed such colorful and
lively designs for your enjoyment.

*Father, thank You for surrounding me with color and life.
Everywhere I look, I see art. Bless You for those who've
taken the time to follow their inspiration and
create great works of beauty. May I never take
their hard work for granted, Lord. Amen.*

95

Music

*Let them praise his name with dancing and
make music to him with timbrel and harp.*
PSALM 149:3 NIV

It rises with majesty as the church organ plays a hymn. It
dances across the keys as the pianist shares her favorite show
tune. It trips across the strings as the guitarist plays an acoustic
melody. Music delights us at every turn. It's such a part of our
lives that we rarely think of it as the gift that it is. The radio in
the car. The sound track to your favorite movie. The children's
choir hard at work. Music uplifts and inspires us. It provides the
sound track to our lives and motivates us to keep going when
we feel like giving up. Today, think of all of the many times and
ways God has used music to lift your spirits. Then thank Him
for the various musicians who made these moments possible.

*Thank You for the gift of music, Father. It livens my day
and draws me closer to You. When I'm down, it lifts me.
When I'm ready to celebrate, it encourages me.
This delightful sound track is very much a part
of who I am, and I'm so grateful for it. Amen.*

Easter

*"They will kill him, and on the third day he will be raised
to life." And the disciples were filled with grief.*
MATTHEW 17:23 NIV

An empty grave. An angelic proclamation. Women in shock.
Disciples reinvigorated with hope. Guards in a state of confusion. These are glimpses of the first Easter Sunday. Can you
picture the expressions on the faces of the women as they ran
to tell the others? Can you imagine the fear in the hearts of the
guards as they conveyed the news to their superiors? The events
of that day were life-changing for all involved, and they changed
the course of history from that day forward. The resurrection
of Jesus brought hope to the hopeless, life to the lifeless, and
joy to those in mourning. It continues to add the perfect plot
twist to literature's most compelling story and changes hearts
in the process. Easter. . .what a gift!

*Easter is my favorite day of the year, Father! It's the day when
I celebrate the resurrection of Your Son. When Jesus came
forth from the tomb, it signaled to all humankind—and to my
heart—that His story was real. Every word He'd spoken was
true. The resurrection sealed the deal both in history and in
my life. I praise You for resurrection Sunday, Father! Amen.*

97

Rainy Days

Ask rain from the LORD in the season of the spring rain, from the LORD who makes the storm clouds, and he will give them showers of rain, to everyone the vegetation in the field.
ZECHARIAH 10:1 ESV

You've settled in with a good book and a cup of hot tea made just the way you like it. Outside, the thunder peals and a streak of lightning illuminates an otherwise dark sky. Before long, the patter of raindrops sounds on the roof, and you can't help but smile. You have no other plans today. Let it rain. You won't be driving in it or making a mad dash across a grocery store parking lot. Not today. You're settled in and comfortable. The soothing sound of drops hitting the awning over the back porch brings back memories of childhood when you donned rain boots and played in puddles. No wandering outside today. Let the kids do that. You have a story to read and feet to elevate. The rain—God's perfect gift for the day—will provide just the backdrop you need to get that done.

Lord, I love the rain! It's soothing, playful, intriguing, and—best of all—it replenishes the earth. What a lovely thing to sit in the comfort of my home while the rain dances all around me. I'm grateful for days like this, Father. Amen.

Passion

*So, whether you eat or drink, or whatever you do,
do all to the glory of God.*
1 CORINTHIANS 10:31 ESV

You know what it's like when the sparkle goes out of a friend's eyes, when the lights dim. You've seen it happen more often than you'd like to admit. It's as if a carefully thought-out gift has been returned to the store because the owner grew weary of it. It's hard to watch passion die. It's even harder when you sense it happening in your own life. Passion is like fuel to a car—it propels things forward. Without it, you drag from task to task, energy waning. Today, ask the Lord to reactivate your passion for Him so that it will spill over into all you say and do. May it propel you at work, home, and play to be all you're created to be. And may it spread like wildfire to those you come into contact with along the way.

I want to be a woman of passion, Father! Light a fire in my heart today. Fan it into flame, and show me how to burn brightly for You. I don't want to go through the motions anymore, Lord. I'm so tired of living like that. From now on, I'll only settle for the real deal—a heart on fire for You. Praise You, Lord! Amen.

99

Positivity

But you must continue to believe this truth and stand
firmly in it. Don't drift away from the assurance you
received when you heard the Good News.
COLOSSIANS 1:23 NLT

Don't you just love positive people? They see the glass as half full no matter how overwhelming the situation. Their eyes are filled with hope, and their speech filled with faith. These beacons of positivity are a reflection of God's heart. He longs for you to remain steadfast, faithful, hopeful. Getting down in the dumps never helped anyone, after all. Squaring your shoulders. Lifting your head. Stepping bravely into the future. . .these are all things God longs for His kids to do, especially when things seem to be against them. So keep a positive outlook. Let that friend rub off on you. Then spread that positivity to others you meet, that their faith might be increased too.

Lord, I want to be a beacon of positivity to those around me,
a true reflection of the kind of hope that comes only
from You. May I shine with God-ordained faith that
others will see Your heart for them. Amen.

100

Adaptability

Do not be conformed to this world, but be transformed by the renewal of your mind, that by testing you may discern what is the will of God, what is good and acceptable and perfect.
ROMANS 12:2 ESV

It is likely that your childhood memories include hours of molding colorful clay or dough into all sorts of shapes. If you didn't like what you'd created, you could mash it up and start over, morphing the dough into something else altogether. Perhaps you even worked with molds, forming all sorts of creative items. The dough was adaptable, able to change. That's how God wants His kids to be. When we're pliable, adaptable, He's able to shape and reshape us into His image. When we get off course, He takes us, much like a potter would take the clay, and begins again. Today, as you think about where you've been and where you're heading, make up your mind to stay pliable in the Potter's hand. He will form you into someone—something—beautiful if you just remain flexible and open to the process.

Lord, thank You for not giving up on me. I want to remain adaptable, pliable in Your hand. Mold me and make me, Father, into a daughter You can be proud of. Amen.

101

Awareness

*Therefore we must pay much closer attention
to what we have heard, lest we drift away from it.*
HEBREWS 2:1 ESV

～

Paying attention. Listening. Watching. Caring. That's what
awareness is. When you find a friend or family member who's
"aware" of your situation, you've found a caring soul, one who's
been keeping watch, even though you didn't realize it. What
about you? Are you aware of your surroundings? Do you know
who's hurting, who's celebrating, and who's barely getting by?
Are you tuned in? Today, ask the Lord to open your eyes to
those who are in need and to open your ears to the cries of
those who need a friend. May you be fully aware of those He's
placed around you so you can minister His great love to them.

*Lord, I'm so grateful for friends who pay attention. I don't
even have to tell them when I'm hurting. They seem to know.
They sweep in and help before I even think to ask. May I be
that kind of friend to others. I want to be aware of what's
going on so I can offer a shoulder to cry on or a hand
up. Slow me down, Father. I don't want to zoom past
people anymore. Increase my awareness
and my love for others, I pray. Amen.*

102

Charisma

*Who gave himself for us to redeem us from all
lawlessness and to purify for himself a people for his
own possession who are zealous for good works.*
TITUS 2:14 ESV

Don't you love charismatic people? They're contagious! They
exude life and radiate joy. Hang around a bubbly, charismatic
person long enough and she'll spill over onto you. There's
something naturally effervescent about her way of viewing
life; you can't help but emulate her. That charisma, her spiritual
power of influence, isn't something she drums up on her own.
It's a God-breathed gift, complete with boundless energy and
the uncanny ability to stir up energy in those she comes in
contact with. Her energy is conferred from on high, straight
from the Lord Himself. She's full of the Spirit of God, an eager
representative of His grace and mercy.

*Lord, I love to see people bubble over with zeal for You.
They inspire me so much. Today I ask You to bless my friends
who exude joy and charisma. Help me to be more like them
and, in doing so, be more like You. Praise You, Father. Amen.*

103

Fairness

Blessed are they who observe justice,
who do righteousness at all times!
PSALM 106:3 ESV

A level playing field. Shared stakes. Equal opportunity. Fairness. Don't you wish the world operated this way? Life would be grand if every job, every family, every sports team operated fairly. Unfortunately, life isn't fair. People knock others down to get to the top rung of the ladder. Teachers play favorites. Coaches prefer one player over another. Even parents sometimes prefer one child over another, giving preferential treatment. But you don't have to live like that. You can treat all people equally and fairly. You can start today, in fact. Don't separate people into categories by race, age, sex, or even by personality. Learn to love them all as God does. In other words, treat them fairly, and you'll be treated fairly in return.

Father, I'll admit, I have my favorites. I sometimes give
preferential treatment. Help me to spread the love, Lord,
and treat everyone fairly, equally. I want to represent
Your heart to all I meet, Lord. Help me? Amen.

104

Optimism

*And we know that for those who love God all things
work together for good, for those who are
called according to his purpose.*
ROMANS 8:28 ESV

A hopeful heart. A smile even in the middle of a storm. A positive word at just the right moment. People who bubble over with optimism have all of these attributes and more. Optimism, at its root, is positivity. When you exude optimism, you lift others up. You encourage. You don't get down in the dumps with every little bump in the road. In fact, you feel called to energize others who are feeling blue. Think of the optimistic people in your world. Have you taken the time to thank them? And what about you? Is the glass half empty or half full? Maybe it's time for God's perspective!

*Lord, I want to be an optimist. Give me eyes to see
situations as You do. I want to encourage others who are
going through hard times just as I've been encouraged by
the optimists in my life. Give me the gift of optimism,
I pray, and I'll use it to bless others! Amen.*

105

Lunch with a Friend

That is, that we may be mutually encouraged
by each other's faith, both yours and mine.
ROMANS 1:12 ESV

Sometimes you just need an hour or two with a friend—time to catch up and share your latest news: your joys, your woes, your frustrations. As you settle in over a yummy meal, all the chaos of the week disappears. Suddenly you're just a friend, ready for a chat. The conversation shifts from kids to relationships to fashion and hair. You're all over the place, but you don't care. That's what friends do. They track with each other. You hang around together until the waitress starts to wonder if you're ever going to leave. Pause to think about the women in your life who have filled the role of friend. How have they blessed you? Have you been that kind of friend to others? It's not too late to start! Pick up the phone and make a lunch date with someone you care about, and then see where the road takes you.

* * *

I love hanging out with friends, Lord. It's great to have one-
on-one time, especially if there's food involved. Help me to
settle in and enjoy these special times without feeling
rushed. I want to be a great friend, Lord.
With Your help, I know I can be. Amen.

106

Thank-You Notes

*Give thanks in all circumstances; for this is the
will of God in Christ Jesus for you.*
1 THESSALONIANS 5:18 ESV

~

Thank-you notes convey sweet, simple messages of the heart,
thanks for little kindnesses. They are usually handwritten on
tiny cards carefully selected for occasions such as this. These
notes are tangible reminders that people still care, that your act
of kindness mattered to someone. These precious notes often
arrive on a day when you least expect them but most need them.
The sender is a conscientious person. She knows just what to
say and how to say it. You wish you had her knack. Or maybe
you do. Maybe you're already a note-sender. You love to thank
people when they've done something sweet to lift your spirits.
Whom will you write to next? Who deserves your thanks? Grab
that pen and start writing!

. . . .

*Lord, You've surrounded me with so many amazing people.
They bless me at every turn. So many times, I forget to thank
the ones who've gone out of their way to bring a smile to my
face. It's time to reciprocate, Father. Show me whom
I can bless today. What little note can I send?
I'll get right on that, Lord! Amen.*

107

Small Things

"One who is faithful in a very little is also faithful in much, and one who is dishonest in a very little is also dishonest in much."
LUKE 16:10 ESV

~

"It's the little things." "The little things mean so much." "God's in the details." "Don't sweat the small stuff." "It's all small stuff." These are likely phrases you've grown to appreciate. Sometimes we forget that God really is in the details. In that smile on the baby's face. In the hot meal your coworker just purchased for you. In the refund you just received from the water company. These might be small when you look at them individually, but add 'em up and you have a whopper of a blessing. Today, make a list of all of the "small" ways you've been touched over the past few days. Add 'em up, and you'll see that God has been hard at work on your behalf, doing all sorts of things to boost your morale and keep your focus on Him. What a gift, these "small" things!

* * *

Father, I see You in all things, big and small. In majestic mountains and in a pile of clean laundry. You're there when I say nighttime prayers with my children and with me in the hospital room when crisis hits. It's easy to get busy and overlook the little blessings You send my way, Lord, but no more! Thank You for the reminder that the small things add up! Amen.

108

Praise

*Let them praise your great
and awesome name! Holy is he!*
PSALM 99:3 ESV

～

We do it at ball games—whoop and holler at the top of our lungs
when our team scores. We do it when our child's first ballet recital
wraps up—carry on with shouts and cheers. We lift hands, hearts,
and voices in joyous praise when we're thrilled and delighted.
And God loves it when we direct praise toward Him as well. In
fact, His Word is filled with scriptures encouraging us to enter
into joyful song, to lift hands in the sanctuary, to fill our hearts
with songs of praise. It's a celebration of the One who created
us. More than just a song or a melody, praise is a gift that rises
up from the core of our being and gushes out like a rushing
waterfall, unencumbered by inhibitions. How long has it been
since you praised with such fierce abandon? Perhaps today's
the day! Enter into His throne room, and lift that voice in praise!

*Father, I praise You! You are so worthy of all of my adoration,
Lord. Maker of all, I honor Your name and bless You for all
You've done and all You are. Praise You, Father. Amen.*

109

Faithful Friend

Greater love has no one than this,
that someone lay down his life for his friends.
JOHN 15:13 ESV

She's not going anywhere. She knows you need her. She needs you too. Through thick and thin, she shows up at your door, sleeves rolled up, ready to get to work on your behalf. She's a faithful friend, one not swayed by flightiness. She's one of those "go the distance" types and has proven it time and time again. And you're so grateful for her. What a gift this stick-to-it friend has been. She's walked you through tragedies, showed up with meals, and stopped by for coffee. . .just because. You couldn't shake her if you wanted to. (Not that you do.) Today, ask the Lord to show you some special way you can honor this precious friend. How can you make her realize that she's one of God's finest gifts to you?

Lord, how You've blessed me through my friends,
especially the ones who show up when I'm in need.
I don't ever want to overlook their kindness, Father.
Help me be the kind of friend that these fine ladies
have been to me. I want to stick close to those who need
me, Lord. Show me how to honor them, I pray. Amen.

110

Brokenness

But he gives more grace. Therefore it says,
"God opposes the proud but gives grace to the humble."
JAMES 4:6 ESV

You're not the woman you used to be. Pieces of you have been broken and mended back together. Your heart has suffered tragedies. You wonder if life on the other side of catastrophe could possibly be as good as what transpired before. You wonder if your heart will ever truly mend. Seasons of brokenness such as this might seem too high a wall to scale, but you will get through it. In fact, brokenness itself can be a gift if you allow it to be. Those moments of shattered frailty cause you to reach out to God as never before, trusting that He, and He alone, can put the pieces together in a way that makes sense. So breathe deeply. Trust. Believe. Mend. He will do the work. Allow Him to begin.

Lord, there are days when I feel so broken I wonder if I will
ever recover. I'm like a shattered plate, pieces too jagged to
glue together. Then You come along, Father, and begin the
piece-work. You mend. You heal. You seal my heart
with Yours, making me stronger than before.
Do Your work in me today, I pray, Lord. Amen.

111

Eternal Life

*For the wages of sin is death, but the gift
of God is eternal life in Christ Jesus our Lord.*
ROMANS 6:23 NIV

Have you pondered the meaning of the word *eternity*? You'll
be held spellbound as you try to figure out how life could go
on and on. . .forever. If you're like most, you view life as finite,
having a beginning and an end. It's almost impossible to fathom
how God's timeline could be so different from our own, but it is.
He has no beginning and no end. (That defies comprehension,
doesn't it?) It's beyond the realm of what we can understand.
Today, ask God to give you His eternal perspective. It's an
amazing gift to see life's circumstances in light of eternity, to
have a "forever" perspective. Suddenly, things that seemed big
will pale in comparison to what's coming. Eternal life is, after
all, the finest gift our heavenly Father has ever given His kids.

*Lord, thank You for inviting me to spend eternity with You.
I want Your eternal perspective, Father. No more getting hung
up on things that have no eternal consequence. From now
on, I want to view my life through Your eyes and
through the lens of eternity. Amen.*

112

Gotcha Gifts

Every good gift and every perfect gift is from above, coming down from the Father of lights, with whom there is no variation or shadow due to change.
JAMES 1:17 ESV

❧

Don't you love "just because" gifts? They come with no rhyme or reason, usually showing up on a day when you're feeling a little blue. They're usually tailored to fit your personality, your talents and abilities, your joys. Best of all, they come from people who know you. . .and know you well. Today, pause to think about all of the "gotcha" gift friends in your circle. What a blessing they are. You've learned from the best. But maybe it's time to reverse things. This time, you send the gift. Choose just the right friend then just the right gift, one guaranteed to bring a smile to her face and a song to her heart. Go on. You know which person to pick. Now get busy and find the right "gotcha," one that she will be talking about for years to come.

Lord, I love my "gotcha" friends. They know me so well. Help me to be that kind of friend to others. I enjoy the element of surprise, so help me come up with the perfect gifts for those I love. What fun we'll have, You and me! Amen.

Blessings in Disguise

For from his fullness we have all received,
grace upon grace.
JOHN 1:16 ESV

It doesn't look like a blessing. It doesn't smell like a blessing. It might not even feel like a blessing. In fact, it feels more like a curse. But that thing you're struggling with might just turn out to be one of the greatest blessings in your life. Oh, you can't see it now. You're still struggling to get through it. But later it will be clear. Your hardest days, your toughest moments are growing you into a woman of God who will be stronger all the way around. Today, take a piece of paper and write the words "Blessings in disguise" on top. Take a close look at all the things you're currently struggling with, and then add those struggles to the list. Come back to your list one month from now, and see how God has moved on your behalf. The struggles will be behind you and blessings will be clear.

Lord, it's hard to imagine that my tough times are going to
produce fruit in my life. Today I ask You to take my hardest
moments and use them for Your glory. Grow me into a woman
who stands firm during rough patches and sees things
the way You do. I praise You in advance for
what You're doing, Father. Amen.

Fellowship

We proclaim to you what we have seen and heard, so that you
also may have fellowship with us. And our fellowship
is with the Father and with his Son, Jesus Christ.
1 JOHN 1:3 NIV

Hanging out. Chatting. Eating. Laughing. Sharing dreams. Playing dominoes. Watching the Super Bowl. Potluck at the church. Sunday school class. Bible study. Women's retreat. Dinner and a movie. These all provide opportunities for fellowship or "friendly association" with those in your circle. When you gather with like-minded people, you can let your guard down, which means you're completely free to have a good time without wondering when or if someone might talk about you behind your back or manipulate you in some way. Perhaps you've allowed yourself to slip away from times of fellowship. Make a list of those you would like to spend time with, and then make it happen. Plan a lunch date. Agree to a Bible study. Buy tickets for a movie. Do all you can to keep those friendships alive and active.

Father, I'll admit I sometimes deliberately move out of
fellowship with like-minded people. I pull away. I feel
weaker during those seasons, Lord. So keep me in the loop.
Show me whom I can trust; then help me put together a plan
to keep "friendly association" at the top of my list. Amen.

Those Who've Gone Before Us

*Therefore, since we are surrounded by so great a cloud of
witnesses, let us also lay aside every weight, and sin which
clings so closely, and let us run with endurance
the race that is set before us.*
HEBREWS 12:1 ESV

Moses. Abraham. Sarah. David. Isaiah. Ruth. Boaz. Job. Hosea.
Matthew. Mark. Luke. John. Peter. Paul. The list of names goes
on and on. When you stop to think about the great men and
women of the Bible who've gone before us, these mighty people
who surround us as a cloud of witnesses to the faith, aren't you
overwhelmed? If they could run their respective races, so can
you. If they could overcome obstacles (especially Job!), so can
you. If they could say, at the end of their days, that the journey
to serve God was the right one for them, then so can you. These
remarkable people are a gift, for they've blazed a trail and taught
us how to serve God, how to live lives worthy of the calling.
What a blessing to have so many examples of godly living. And
what a thrill to be grafted into that great family, the family of God.

*Father, I'm surrounded on every side! Men and women of
yesteryear, my grandparents, great-grandparents, and so
on. . .so many of these wonderful people devoted their lives
to You. They've taught me how to live, Lord, and I want to
follow in their footsteps. Thank You for grafting
me into the family, Father. Amen.*

116

God's Calling

For God's gifts and his call are irrevocable.
ROMANS 11:29 NIV

You have the unmistakable sense that you're supposed to do something, to head in a particular direction. Something is driving you to take steps toward that dream. Is it possible God is calling you to do something new, exciting, brave? God often calls His kids to step out of their comfort zones and follow Him into new areas, but what is a "calling" exactly? First, we're called to know Him more, to spend time at His feet. In that special place, He reveals plans, destiny, dreams to our hearts. Think of these things as a destination, some place you're pointed toward. He won't force you to move in the direction of your calling, but the more time you spend with Him, the more you will want to please His heart. Today, picture the Lord summoning you to do something great with Him. Will you take steps in that direction?

Lord, thank You for showing me in our time together that You have a call on my life, a destiny, a hope, a future. I want to step out, Father. Give me courage to go where You call me to go and do what You've called me to do. I love You, Lord! Amen.

Words

Let the words of my mouth and the meditation of my heart be acceptable in your sight, O LORD, my rock and my redeemer.
PSALM 19:14 ESV

We use them by the thousands each day. They tear down. They build up. They are long, short, hyphenated, shrill, calm, slow, fast, and loaded with punch. They are our words, and they're weapons in our hands, usable for good or evil. The gift of speech is just that…a gift. Can you imagine going through life with no way of expressing yourself? This is a very special gift from our heavenly Father, because we get to use our own creative powers to string together the words of our choice as we meander our way through life's ups and downs. How carefully have you chosen your words today? Have you given them much thought? Why not take the time to look at your words as a special gift? Make sure their delivery is pleasant and their tone sweet. Most of all, commit them to God that they might be acceptable in His sight.

Father, I want to choose my words with great care so that they build others up. May I never use them in a way that would bring harm to those around me or to You. I commit my words to You today, Lord. Speak through me, I pray. Amen.

118

Good Times and Bad

*And let us not grow weary of doing good, for in due
season we will reap, if we do not give up.*
GALATIANS 6:9 ESV

There will be bad times. Maybe you don't like to read those
words. You're one of those "let the good times roll" sorts who
closes her eyes to the bad. But if everything was rosy, how
would growth start? Yes, there will be bad times. You will be
hurt. Falsely accused. Wounded by friends. But there will also
be amazing times. You'll fall in love. Care for little ones. Get
promotions at work. The good and bad balance as time goes
on. The key to successful living is to not give up during the
low times and to not take credit for the good times. Most of all,
be consistent in your walk with Christ. You will reap a great
reward if you don't give up.

*Lord, it's been tempting to give up at times. You've seen how
low my lows have been during the rough seasons. But I'm
learning that the good times really do make up for them.
For every low, there's a high. Keep me focused on You, Lord,
that I can be consistent in good times and bad. Amen.*

Values

"No one can serve two masters, for either he will hate the one and love the other, or he will be devoted to the one and despise the other. You cannot serve God and money."
MATTHEW 6:24 ESV

Principles. Standards. The things you hold dear. These are your values. You care deeply about them to the point of drawing lines in the sand so that you don't cross over to the other side. Maybe you have deep, abiding beliefs based on your interpretation of scripture. Perhaps you're passionate about purity. Maybe you have made up your mind not to swear or see movies you deem inappropriate. Others don't always agree or understand, but you're determined to stick with it. This is your personal moral code, your standard, and you'll live within the confines of it. Today, take a look at your life values. They are a gift of sorts. God has given you these values to protect you and to bring joy, life, and satisfaction.

Lord, I've rarely stopped to consider my values, the things I feel strongly about. Reaffirm the things that are important both to Your heart and mine so I can strengthen my resolve. I want to live within the boundaries that You create, God, even if others don't agree or understand. I need Your help, Father. Amen.

120

Clean Sheets

In peace I will both lie down and sleep;
for you alone, O Lord, make me dwell in safety.
PSALM 4:8 ESV

❧

They're crisp. They're comfortable. They smell fabulous. Clean sheets make everything feel better. No matter how difficult your day, when you slide into bed and pull those soft, cool sheets up, all is right with the world. For that moment, you're cocooned in a blissful state, ready to drift off to sleep. The cares of the world melt away, replaced by inexplicable comfort. Today, as you think about the comfort of those sheets, pause to pray for those who are homeless, who are sleeping without the benefits of a cozy mattress or fresh, clean sheets. Then, after you've prayed, take action! Find a local shelter and donate sheets and blankets for those in need. Talk about a lovely covering!

Father, I love that feeling I get when I settle in for the
night. Those crisp, clean sheets feel (and smell!) so good.
Thank You for the reminder that I can help "cover" those in
need by providing to a local shelter. Help me as I figure out
the details, Lord. I want to be a blessing, Lord. Amen.

121

Pets

Whoever is righteous has regard for the life of his beast,
but the mercy of the wicked is cruel.
PROVERBS 12:10 ESV

⤳

They cuddle up next to us. Their funny antics make us laugh. They kiss away our tears and provide comfort when we're grieving. Pets are, perhaps, one of the finest gifts God has ever provided for humankind. Maybe you can relate. That special dog or cat has been with you for years. You don't know what you'd do without her. She was there when you walked through the death of your mother. She stuck with you when you went through that awful breakup. She's greeted you at the door every evening after work for as long as you can remember. Sure, she misbehaves at times, but that little doll is as much a part of your family as anyone, and you're so grateful for her. Today, take the time to thank God for these amazing pets.

God, I'm so grateful for my pets. Each one has been so
special. Loneliness is a thing of the past when I have that
little cuddle-bug next to me. Thank You for making sure
I have a companion, Lord, one with four paws. Amen.

122

Stars

He determines the number of the stars;
he gives to all of them their names.
PSALM 147:4 ESV

They twinkle above you at night, reminding you of the vastness of the universe. They are the subject of nursery rhymes, children's songs, and delightful stories. Strung together with invisible thread, they make up constellations. We can observe the Little Dipper, the Great Bear, and many other imaginative designs. Stars are a gift because they keep our imagination alive and remind us that Someone Else is out there, at work in the great beyond. His ways are higher, brighter, more creative than anything we could dream up for ourselves. Tonight, before your head hits the pillow, take the time to go outside and look at the stars. Really look at them. See them through childlike eyes. Then take the time to thank God for including you in His great, vast plan.

Lord, I love to gaze at the stars. They always make me think
of You. I can imagine Your fingertips spinning them all
into space. Thank You for the reminder that this great,
vast universe is all under Your control, Father.
You created it all and included me in Your
plan. Thank You for that! Amen.

123

Sunshine After Rain

From the rising of the sun to its setting, the name of
the LORD is to be praised!
PSALM 113:3 ESV

Don't you just love a bright, sunny day? No matter what problems you're facing, sunshine can change your perspective. It literally switches the light on and gives you hope where there's been no hope. Perhaps there's no greater time to enjoy the sun than right after a storm. When you've faced something dark, bleak, scary, you can get overwhelmed. Then the sun peeks through. Before long, your spirits have lifted, your courage is restored, and you're ready to face a new day. In many ways, hope is like the sunshine after the rain. It lifts our spirits and gives us courage to keep going. It lights our way. Aren't you grateful for new possibilities?

Lord, I love a good rain shower, but I'm always ready for the
sun to shine through when it's over. Just as hope dries my
tears, the sun dries up the land and lights our way.
Thank You for that reminder, Father. I want to move
forward with the light switch turned on! Amen.

124

Grassy Fields

For behold, the winter is past; the rain is over and gone.
The flowers appear on the earth, the time of singing has come,
and the voice of the turtledove is heard in our land.
SONG OF SOLOMON 2:11–12 ESV

They stretch before you like an endless possibility. . .grassy fields freshly mowed, with that heavenly scent only God could have created. There's just something about a wide-open space that beckons you, calls you out to play. You want to run through it barefoot, to roll around like you did as a child. It signifies that all is well. The rains have come. Grass is growing. Flowers are blooming. Those dried, unproductive fields are a thing of the past. Hope has been restored. All the signs are there. You can lift your head and look toward the future. Today (if you're able), get outside. Spend time in nature. Then ask God to open doors of possibility for your future.

Lord, I love getting outside and spending time with You.
I really enjoy being out on the land, Father. It stretches
wide and seems to call my name. Today I thank You for the
reminder that You're the giver of hope and possibilities.
Take me where You want me to go, Lord, even if it's
into the vast unknown. I trust You, Lord. Amen.

125

Aroma of Flowers

I am a rose of Sharon, a lily of the valleys.
SONG OF SOLOMON 2:1 ESV

The aroma of freshly cut roses is an intoxicating thing. Their scent has you bending down and sniffing the blossoms. The finest, most expensive perfume can't compare to the luscious scent God has placed in the vast array of flowers that bloom in the springtime. Talk about sheer delight! They are signs of things to come. Can you even imagine what heaven will smell like? Perhaps every corridor will have a different aroma. Maybe the scents will be tailored to each person's likes. Wouldn't that be amazing? The point is, God cares so much about us that He even provided lovely scents for us to enjoy. So why not pick up some fresh flowers today? They'll bring a smile to your face and a lovely fragrance to your home.

I love freshly cut flowers, Lord. They make my heart sing.
Thank You for the reminder that You care about every
aspect of my life, even the scents I enjoy. You're a
God of details. I love that about You, Lord!
Thank You for caring so much. Amen.

126

Blue Skies

When I look at your heavens, the work of your fingers,
the moon and the stars, which you have set in place,
what is man that you are mindful of him,
and the son of man that you care for him?
PSALM 8:3-4 ESV

The sky hovers over you in the most thrilling shade of blue you've ever seen. In fact, it's so clear, so pristine, that you almost think it's a painting, not the real deal. You stare up, up, up, wondering how this day could be any more perfect. Blue skies have you singing a song of joy, for they represent unlimited possibilities. They make you want to soar like an eagle, your visibility unlimited. They also remind you that God has you covered. No matter what you're facing, He's surrounding you on all sides. Like a brightly covered canvas, He's painting new possibilities for you. So go ahead. Gaze at the breathtaking sky above. Let it take you to places yet unseen. Soar on wings of eagles and imagine all that God has planned for you.

Lord, thank You for blue skies. They're wide open to possibilities.
They remind me that all is well. No dark clouds hovering.
No storm on the way. Just peace. Solitude. Beauty. I feel like
spreading my wings and setting to flight on days like this,
Father! I'm also reminded of Your covering, Your provision.
Thank You for all You're doing in my life. Amen.

127

Going Barefoot

How beautiful upon the mountains are the feet of him who brings good news, who publishes peace, who brings good news of happiness, who publishes salvation, who says to Zion, "Your God reigns."
ISAIAH 52:7 ESV

Oh, those glorious barefoot days of spring and summer. You love the feel of the grass against the soles of your feet. It tickles and soothes and reminds you of your childhood when you would skip and play with your siblings and friends. Bare feet are a symbol, really, that you are unencumbered, free from the burdens of the day. There's no reason to slip on those shoes, because you have no big plans. This is a cozy day, a stay-home-and-play day. It's a day when you're free to worship God, to proclaim, "Our God reigns!" So what's keeping you? Kick off those shoes and spend some time in His presence.

Lord, I love those barefoot days! They don't come often enough for me. Thanks for letting me walk barefoot in the grass where I'm transported back to the days of my childhood. What precious memories await me on days such as this. I'm so grateful. Amen.

128

Unexpected Bouquet of Flowers

The flowers appear on the earth,
the time of singing has come.
SONG OF SOLOMON 2:12 ESV

✧

They arrive unexpectedly, their radiant colors and intoxicating aromas delighting you at once. You scoop the bouquet into your arms and make your way to the kitchen where you locate the perfect vase. Minutes later, the flowers take center stage on the kitchen table, a public display of your loved one's affection for you. Those flowers represent more than a gift; they are a symbol of love, of relationship. You're not sure what you did to deserve them, but you wouldn't send them back to the florist's shop for anything. They're yours now, and you plan to enjoy them. Looking at them gives you an idea. If someone could take the time to send you flowers, perhaps you could do the same for someone else. . .keep the gift going, as it were. Whom will you send them to? Well, that's up to you!

Lord, thank You for creating a wide variety of flowers.
And thank You for the many times You've whispered,
"Buy those for her," to my friend or loved one's heart.
What a precious gift, Lord. Now, please help
me decide whom I can bless, Father. Amen.

129

Graduates

Being confident of this, that he who began a good work in you
will carry it on to completion until the day of Christ Jesus.
PHILIPPIANS 1:6 NIV

She's done the work. She's poured herself out, taking test after
test. And now that hard work has paid off. It's time to graduate,
to transition from one stage of life to another. You're there for
her, celebrating as she moves the tassel from one side of her cap
to the other. And you're about to bust your buttons because you
know what it's taken to get her to this point. She's your pride
and joy, and her future is filled with endless possibilities. As
you watch her cross that stage, your heart wants to burst into
song. Graduation signifies a good-bye to yesterday and hello to
the next phase of life. There's a bit of sadness associated with
that notion, but you'll get through it. Joy will see you through.

Lord, thank You for the reminder that graduation is a symbol
of transitioning from one stage of life to another. I'm so proud
of all my loved ones who are taking this next big step.
They've worked so hard. I truly believe the best is yet to
come with Your guidance, and I'm trusting that You
have their futures in Your hands. Amen.

130

Good Influences

*You were running well. Who hindered you from obeying
the truth? This persuasion is not from him who calls
you. A little leaven leavens the whole lump.*
GALATIANS 5:7–9 ESV

When you stop to think about the people your children hang
out with, do you pause and pray for good influences? With so
many things tugging at them, kids need friends who will lead
them in the right direction. These wonderful people—the ones
who could be going along with the crowd but choose to stand
firm in their beliefs—are God-sent. They're a gift from the Lord,
a testimony. God sends them at just the right time, when their
influence is most powerful. What a gift they are! And while
you're praying for good influences, pray also that your children
will shine their lights brightly while at school and play. This
world needs all the light it can get, after all.

*Father, thank You for interrupting my son or daughter's life
to bring a friend of godly influence. I pray that You will
bless this child. And Lord, please touch my child that
they might reach others for You. I praise You
in advance for their testimonies, Lord. Amen.*

131

Moral Compass

In all your ways submit to him,
and he will make your paths straight.
PROVERBS 3:6 NIV

⁓

There are those who, led by the Spirit, always seem to point themselves toward true north. They don't waver. They fix their eyes on the goal, the prize set before them, and march ahead, undeterred by temptations on every side. They can be found in schools, jobsites, churches, neighborhoods, and even in Washington, DC. They are active in sports, entertainment, and in the political arena. Today, as you set out on your journey, thank God for that inward moral compass, the conviction of the Holy Spirit. It is a gift, one meant to guide you with determination and passion toward a stronger, healthier relationship with your heavenly Father. No distractions for you! Keep your eye on the prize, and march on.

* *

Father, thank You for my moral compass. It serves as a guide
and always points me toward You. I don't ever want to
leave the path You've set before me. May my eyes
always be fixed on You, Lord, as I continue
to take steps in Your direction. Amen.

132

Full Moon

*And God made the two great lights—the greater light
to rule the day and the lesser light to rule the night—
and the stars.*
GENESIS 1:16 ESV

That lovely golden orb hovering in the night sky serves as an ever-present reminder that God is infinite and Creator of all. Just as the surface of the moon reflects the brilliant light of the sun, God's children are called to be a reflection of the One who spun all things into existence. More than anything, the moon serves as a light on an otherwise dark night, illuminating the path in front of us so we don't lose our way. May we, as children of the King, light the path for a watching world so others can be guided toward our wonderful Creator. We want to point others to Him so they can walk in the light as well. What a beautiful reflection He's called us to be.

*Lord, I want to reflect Your brilliance so others will be
drawn to You. May I shine with such love, such affection,
that I truly reflect Your heart for those around
me. Use me, Father, I pray. Amen.*

133

A Carefully Delivered Message

By the word of the LORD the heavens were made,
and by the breath of his mouth all their host.
PSALM 33:6 ESV

They lift you up, bring you down, pat you on the back, stab you in the heart. Words have power. That's why it's so important to use them as a gift to bless others. How do we do this? We should choose our words carefully, of course, but tone is also critical. We should think carefully about how each word should be delivered before it ever leaves our mouths. Even a tough message can be delivered in love. Words are a precious gift, specially delivered on a silver platter to the one you're speaking to. Those words should bring safety. Love. Hope. They should be carefully delivered, not spoken in anger or rashness. May they bless and uplift others so that they too are encouraged to speak words of life straight from the heart.

Lord, I want to bless others with my carefully thought-out words. Please forgive me for the many times I've used them as weapons instead of instruments of grace. My delivery has been hurtful at times, and I'm so sorry. May my speech be a reflection of Your heart, Father. Amen.

134

Fresh Air

Let everything that has breath
praise the LORD! Praise the LORD!
PSALM 150:6 ESV

Don't you love traveling to the mountains or the seaside? Free from the walls that shield you at home to draw breath after breath of fresh, clean air. It's crisp. It's cool. It's different somehow. In this special place, you breathe easier. Your cares are lifted. In the same manner, your life can be a breath of fresh air to those you hang out with. When you walk in the room, they should sense the Holy Spirit in you. It's fresh, clean, crisp. It's inviting, invigorating, and loving. Today, choose to be that breath of fresh air to your friends. May they sense God's love in you in word and action.

I love getaways, Lord, especially those that steady my breathing. May I be a person who brings that same sense of refreshment to my friends and loved ones. I want to blow in like a holy wind, encouraging change, inviting kindness, stirring love. Help me be a breath of fresh air, Lord. Amen.

Ideas

For we are his workmanship, created in Christ Jesus
for good works, which God prepared beforehand,
that we should walk in them.
EPHESIANS 2:10 ESV

You're struck with one just as you're falling asleep. If you don't write it down, you might forget. Another one hits when you're in the shower. No way to scribble something down in here—pass the bath crayons, please!—so you'll have to do your best not to forget. Your best one yet comes as you're driving the kids to school. Ideas come at the strangest times, don't they? Theory has it, they strike when you're the most relaxed. (Maybe it's time to keep a pen and paper on your bedside table!) If you're a creative, right-brained thinker, you might be loaded with ideas. You have far too many to act on. Ask God to show you which ones are meant to stick. If ideas don't come easily to you, ask the Lord to stir your creative juices and for His Spirit to hover over you as it did during creation. He will do it! You are created in the image of your (very!) creative Father, after all.

I'm so glad I have your creative DNA, Father! Sometimes I
feel like ideas are flowing by the minute. Not every "amazing
idea" will come to fruition, but I thank You for the possibility
to dream, to imagine, to wonder. How I love seeing
the finest ones come to pass! Amen.

136

Stillness

"I have told you these things, so that in me you may have peace. In this world you will have trouble. But take heart! I have overcome the world."
JOHN 16:33 NIV

There's something rather exquisite about the stillness, isn't there? No honking horns or blaring televisions. No voices raised in anger or text messages beeping. No hustling or bustling as people run from here to there. Just the bliss of peaceful nothingness. Of course, this world doesn't provide many opportunities for stillness. That's why it's important to sneak away from time to time. Even if you have to sit in your car for a few moments without the radio blaring or take a bubble bath without the kids screaming from the other side of the bathroom door, do what you can to enter into quietness from time to time. When the noises shut down, you're better able to hear the voice of God as He whispers sweet nothings in your ear. *Shh.* Do you hear it?

Lord, how I love sitting in the stillness with You, where the only voice I hear is Yours. There, in that quiet place, I'm free to settle my thoughts, to remain still and peaceful. I can lay down my worries and my hurries. . .and just be. Thank You for that quiet, peaceful refuge, Father. It's such a gift. Amen.

137

Long Conversations

Walk with the wise and become wise,
for a companion of fools suffers harm.
PROVERBS 13:20 NIV

Some conversations go on for hours. You don't plan them in advance. You don't make a list of topics ahead of time. They just flow naturally, like a river rushing over the rocks, headed downstream. By the time several hours have passed, you're both astounded. How did that happen? Quite naturally, of course. When you find someone safe, someone who hears your heart and responds with godly wisdom, laughter, and encouraging words, it's easy to keep the conversation going. When you think of a friend who loves long chats, who comes to mind? Maybe it's time to pick up the phone and call her. You're probably both overdue for a good, long conversation.

Father, I'm so grateful for friends who engage me in
comfortable conversation. What a gift they are. They listen.
I listen. They share. I share. We move our stories forward
with comfort and ease. Thank You for these precious
people, Lord. Don't ever let me forget how
much we need each other. Amen.

138

Time

*So teach us to number our days that we
may get a heart of wisdom.*
PSALM 90:12 ESV

A second, a minute, an hour, a day, a week, a month, a year. We've laid out our clock and calendar accordingly. In many cases we've marked up every day, down to the minute. We're booked. . .and exhausted. Isn't it remarkable to know God's definition of time is different from ours? To Him, a thousand years is like a day, and a day is like a year. No matter what you have on your busy schedule, take a moment to thank God for the gift of time. He's given you twenty-four hours a day to live a full life and to make a difference in this world. He's placed you here on the planet at exactly the right time in history so you can impact those around you at exactly the time He's designed. Remarkable, right? So use your time wisely.

*Lord, I'm so grateful for the gift of time. You have
things for me to do, but You're not rushing me to the
goal. You're gracious and gentle with me. I do want
to make a difference, Father, no matter how long
it takes. Thank You for using me, Lord. Amen.*

Accepting Yourself

Then God said, "Let us make mankind in our image,
in our likeness, so that they may rule over the fish in the
sea and the birds in the sky, over the livestock and
all the wild animals, and over all the creatures
that move along the ground."
GENESIS 1:26 NIV

The face stares back at you in the mirror. You can't bear to look at the wrinkles, the double chin. You turn sideways to look at your profile then groan as you notice the protruding belly and saggy upper arms. This isn't the image you'd hoped to see, but it's your reality. How did it come to this? For a minute you're tempted to despair, then just as quickly you shift gears. Who cares if your skin is wrinkly or your midsection rounded? Why not just enjoy the body you've been given and thank God that you're healthy and alive? For that matter, why not accept that you're okay just as you are? Accepting yourself, loving yourself as Christ loves you, is so vital to your mental and emotional health. It's also important to your spiritual health. After all, if you're so busy beating yourself up, you don't have much time left to thank the One who created you in the first place.

Lord, I'm tired of beating myself up. I'm ready to get on with
the task of loving myself in spite of my flaws. Please forgive
me for being so self-absorbed, for caring too much about
this outer shell, Father. Help me, I pray. Amen.

140

Old Friends

*Two are better than one, because they have a good return for
their labor: if either of them falls down, one can help the other
up. But pity anyone who falls and has no one to help them up.*
ECCLESIASTES 4:9–10 NIV

❧

You rarely get to see them, but they're as dear to you as ever.
Friends from long ago have settled into your heart, occupying
a comfortable space no one else can fill. You're awash with
memories as their names are mentioned and tickled pink
when you hear from them again. Your relationship with these
special ones spans decades and will go on for many years to
come, whether you find time to meet in person or not. What a
precious gift these fine people are, like jewels in a crown that
has stood the test of time.

*Lord, You've blessed me with great friends over the years.
Many are still a part of my life, active in my goings-on.
Others I haven't seen for years, but I know they pray for
me and care about what I'm facing. For those who are
far away, Father, I pray a blessing. May they know how
deeply they are loved and how grateful I am for
the role they have played in my life. Amen.*

141

Text Messaging

A word fitly spoken is like apples
of gold in a setting of silver.
PROVERBS 25:11 ESV

Oh, the joy of sending and receiving instantaneous messages. The ability to connect with someone at lightning speed is more than just handy; it can be a lifesaver. It's also a great way to stay in touch with loved ones who live on the other side of the country or even the other side of the world. Text messaging might get a bad rap because it's not as personal as a face-to-face meeting, but it's a terrific way to let people know what's going on in your life and vice versa. The ability to send pictures, videos, and words of encouragement—and all at the push of a button—is truly a twenty-first-century gift, one meant to bind us together with those we love.

Lord, I'm grateful for instant communication. It has come in
handy so many times. That little "ding" on my phone lets me
know that someone cares, someone wants to stay in touch.
May I never take for granted this marvelous technology,
for it keeps me in the loop no matter how
far away I might be. Amen.

Open Communication

A soft answer turns away wrath,
but a harsh word stirs up anger.
PROVERBS 15:1 ESV

No hiding. No tucking things away into cobwebbed corners. Everything out in the open. That's the best way to live. And when you find someone who's willing to share openly with you—even if the openness carries a sting—you've found a true gift. Of course, it's not always easy to live this way. We don't always want to hear what others have to say—especially when it's about us. We often don't want to take the time to listen to their struggles and worries either. We're too busy for all that. Some of us aren't accustomed to vulnerability from others or ourselves. So, what do people say about you? Do they see you as an open book or a closed door? Do you hide away, praying no one sees your struggles, your failures? Today is the best possible day to open up to a friend. Don't worry about rejection. Ask God to show you people who can be trusted, and then gently nudge that door open.

Lord, I know that confession is good for the soul.
There are many times I need someone to share my
burdens with. Help me as I open the door, Father.
I want to step through with Your help. Amen.

143

Birthdays

For by me your days will be multiplied,
and years will be added to your life.
PROVERBS 9:11 ESV

~⁓~

Cake. Candles. Presents. These are the images of another year's passage—your birthday. Every year that cycles around to meet the next is worthy of celebration, for it indicates the obvious: you've made it this far! Woo-hoo! Congratulations! Birthdays are indeed a gift, a reminder of the life God has given us and a celebration of time spent with those we love. Instead of bemoaning your next birthday, play it up! Have a party to end all parties. Kick up your heels. Let the world know just how happy you are to be alive and well and how excited you are about the days ahead. Your birthday is a gift not just to yourself but to all who love you.

* * *

Lord, I don't always like to admit my age. Sometimes I feel it
acutely. Please forgive me for moaning and groaning about
all the years that have passed. Thank You for the reminder
that life is a gift. Birthdays are a lovely reminder of that,
and I plan to celebrate with abandon next
time around. Praise You, Father. Amen.

144

Bubble Baths

*"Come to me, all you who are weary and burdened,
and I will give you rest."*
MATTHEW 11:28 NIV

A mountain of frothy white bubbles rising above the edge of the tub. Warm, sudsy water. That luxurious feeling you get as you settle in and rest your head against the bath pillow. Ah, bubble baths! Can anything compare? For those quiet, peaceful moments, you are totally relaxed, mind and heart calm. All the cares of the day are suddenly washed away, replaced with peace, joy, reflection. You're finally able to still your racing thoughts and simply be. There, in that set-apart place, every problem vanishes, every fear disappears. Sure, you'll eventually have to get back out of the tub, but for now every trouble vanishes under a sea of foamy bubbles. What a gift this glorious me-time can be.

*Father, thank You for set-apart times when I can simply relax.
My life is so hectic, and it feels good to soak my troubles away
in that warm, sudsy water. I'm so grateful for the peace that
comes during those precious alone times, Lord. Amen.*

145

A Baby's Birth

"I prayed for this child, and the LORD has granted me
what I asked of him. So now I give him to the LORD.
For his whole life he will be given over to the
LORD." And he worshiped the LORD there.
1 SAMUEL 1:27–28 NIV

She enters the world, pink and vibrant, her lungs releasing the first whoosh of air as she announces, "I'm here!" You stare in awe at this miracle, this newborn angel, this perfect baby doll, afraid to touch her for fear she'll break. And yet you must take her into your arms. She has just landed on earth from heaven, after all, a gift wrapped up in ribbons and bows. You coo and babble, ready to win her over with your broad smile and entertaining giggles as you touch her tiny nose. Oh, this beautiful gift! Only minutes old, and she has won your heart already. Will you ever be the same?

Lord, the miracle of childbirth exceeds anything I can
imagine. How did you come up with the concept, Father?
Was the plan meant to delight us on every level, to show us
glimpses of heaven in advance? We are wowed as new life
emerges, Lord. Praise You for the miracle of birth! Amen.

146

Vehicles

The LORD will keep your going out and your coming
in from this time forth and forevermore.
PSALM 121:8 ESV

They come in all shapes and sizes and in every price range.
From tiny sports cars to midsized sedans to oversized SUVs,
the roads are full of vehicles buzzing here and there. Inside,
single folks, families, people on their way to work, school, and
play. Where would this world be without vehicles? How would
we get from here to there? Modern transportation is a wonderful gift, one we often take for granted. Imagine a life with no
transportation! Today, take the time to thank the Lord for your
vehicle or mode of transportation. He makes sure you get to
the places you need to go.

I know You care about my comings and goings, Lord.
Your Word says so. And I know You care about how I get
there. Thank You for the many vehicles you've sent
my way over the years. You always provide,
Lord, and I'm very grateful. Amen.

A Good Night's Sleep

If you lie down, you will not be afraid;
when you lie down, your sleep will be sweet.
PROVERBS 3:24 ESV

Is there anything sweeter than resting your head against the pillow and feeling the weight of sleep pull your eyelids down, down, down? Or that lovely twilight moment when you're half-awake, half-asleep, and the tug-of-war ceases as you give yourself over to slumber. Perhaps the only thing finer is to awaken the following morning feeling refreshed and new, ready to face the day ahead of you. This is only made possible by a good night's sleep, something we often take for granted. Have you considered the notion that sleep is a gift? Even the Lord took a break, after all. He initiated the Sabbath, a day of rest from His creative efforts. He loves to see you refreshed and rejuvenated, so don't fight it! Climb into bed and close those eyes. Tomorrow is a new day filled with possibilities, but you can only experience them fully if you've had a good night's sleep.

Lord, thank You for giving me the time I need to rest.
After my crazy whirl-about days, I need to sleep.
What a wonderful feeling, to wake up refreshed,
ready to face the day. Thank You, Father. Amen.

148

Helpers

But if we walk in the light, as he is in the light,
we have fellowship with one another, and the blood
of Jesus his Son cleanses us from all sin.
1 JOHN 1:7 ESV

Whew! You can't do it all on your own, can you? You've tried and tried, but it's just not happening. Deadlines aren't being met. The house is a wreck. The kids are hungry. Your husband's wondering if he's ever going to have alone time with you. You're wiped out, and rightfully so. You have too much on your plate. Time to call in the cavalry, my friend! There are people in the wings just waiting to help. In fact, a few of them were wondering if you were ever going to ask. They have the skills. They have the time. They have the know-how. So don't hesitate. Ask for—and receive—help. And while you're at it, usher up a prayer of thanks for these fine people. They've been knocking at your door for a while, wondering if or when you might open it.

I'm sorry it's taken me so long to ask for help, Lord.
You know how I am. . . . I like to do things on my own.
Thank You for sending qualified people my way, Father.
I want to draw close to them so that we can learn
from each other. Today I humble myself, Lord. Amen.

149

Dishwashers

For a day in your courts is better than a thousand elsewhere. I would rather be a doorkeeper in the house of my God than dwell in the tents of wickedness.
PSALM 84:10 ESV

~⚬~

Picture the housewife of the 1940s, washing, rinsing, and drying every dish by hand. She couldn't picture doing it any other way. Then, in the 1950s, along came the dishwasher. It must've seemed too good to be true: "All I have to do is set my dishes in that machine and it does all the work?" How marvelous to step away and rest while the dishes were made squeaky-clean by then-modern technology. Though it might seem silly to list dishwashers under the heading of "gifts," they are, indeed. They speed up our lives and give us more time to spend with those we love. So instead of griping about how long it takes to load and unload, usher up a prayer of thanks that the modern way is the easier way.

Lord, sometimes I forget that people in my lifetime—my grandparents, aunts, uncles, and so on—didn't have the conveniences I now enjoy. Thank You for every modern marvel, for each one represents more time I can spend with my family. Amen.

150

Saturdays

So God blessed the seventh day and made it holy,
because on it God rested from all his work
that he had done in creation.
GENESIS 2:3 ESV

You need it. You deserve it. You've earned it. Saturday's coming, and you can't wait. It's an "other than" day, a day you can plan outings, a trip to the grocery store, phone calls to loved ones, and so on. Anything "other than" your day job. So what are you planning this Saturday? Maybe you want to lounge around the house. Maybe it's time to do laundry or vacuum. Perhaps you have big plans for a date with your husband or a getaway with your Bible study group. Maybe you're taking the kids to the pool or going to the movies with a friend. The world (er, day) is your oyster! Whatever you have on your plate, thank God for the freedom to do it on this set-apart day, one meant for rest, refreshment, and regeneration.

Lord, I love Saturdays. It frees me to know that even You took
a day off, Father. If You needed the rest, I'm sure I do
too. I'm grateful for the time to refresh before I have
to start my work week over again. Thanks for
thinking of time off, Lord! Amen.

151

Living within Your Means

For each will have to bear his own load.
GALATIANS 6:5 ESV

❧

Life provides temptations a-plenty. Chief among them is the desire to spend beyond your means. You see the perfect-for-you dress hanging on a rack at the store. The price tag causes you to swallow hard, but it is, after all, perfect. So you purchase it. This trend continues as the days, weeks, months, years move on until you reach a point where credit card debt begins to swallow you whole. At this point you come to the realization that living within your means is more than a clever idea conjured up by some Scrooge who doesn't want you to have a good time—it's an absolute necessity in life, a gift, even. So you readjust your thinking, and the story has a happily-ever-outcome, all because you accepted the gift of living within your means. Now, this is one gift you can happily give yourself!

Thank You, Father, for the reminder that my needs and wants are two separate things. Show me how to walk past the temptations and live completely within my means so I can bring honor to You in all I do. Amen.

152

Family

"But if serving the LORD seems undesirable to you, then choose for yourselves this day whom you will serve, whether the gods your ancestors served beyond the Euphrates, or the gods of the Amorites, in whose land you are living. But as for me and my household, we will serve the LORD."
JOSHUA 24:15 NIV

Perhaps there's no greater time to enjoy your family than in the summertime. Those long, hot days are made sweeter by vacations, trips to the swimming pool, picnics under the oak tree, day trips to amusement parks, and visits to family friends. And while every day of summer might not be perfect, at least you'll be together, one big, happy family. Today, why not make a list of some summer activities you can do with those you love. How can you surprise the little ones? How can you bring a smile to the face of a sibling, parent, or grown child? God has given you this remarkable family unit to enjoy. There's no greater time than now!

Lord, I'm so grateful for my family members. We have so many great roads to travel together. Show us where You want us to go, Lord. Lead the way and I'll follow, my hand in theirs. Thank You for the gift of family, Father. Amen.

Children

These commandments that I give you today are to be on your hearts. Impress them on your children. Talk about them when you sit at home and when you walk along the road, when you lie down and when you get up. Tie them as symbols on your hands and bind them on your foreheads. Write them on the doorframes of your houses and on your gates.
DEUTERONOMY 6:6–9 NIV

Children are a gift from the Lord, wrapped up in all sorts of different ribbons and bows. Each child is unique with his or her own footprint and imprint on our heart. Whether this child comes to us biologically or through adoption (or as a godchild, niece, nephew, and so on), we're smitten. We slip into mama-bear mode right away, ready to protect, defend, and tend to. No matter what we face as these kiddos grow up—dealing with everything from skinned knees, to broken bones, sibling rivalry and messy bedrooms—they're worth it. Yes, they're even worth it during those volatile teenage years! Children are our legacy, our loves, and our lives. They are heaven-sent and filled with possibilities.

Father, thank You for the children in my life. I love them all. Show me how to be the best parent, grandparent, aunt, or friend I can be. I know these little ones will mirror me, Lord, so I want to be a reflection of You in all I do. Help me, I pray. Amen.

154

Fun Moments

Delight yourself in the LORD;
and He will give you the desires of your heart.
PSALM 37:4 NASB

Aren't you glad the word *delight* is in the Bible? God wants us to delight ourselves in Him. That means He's a delightful Father! Can you picture it now, a daddy playing with his little girl? Lifting her in the air, swinging her around until she squeals with glee. That's the sort of playfulness and carefree living God wants you to feel when you come into His presence. Instead of being fearful that He will reject you because of a mistake you've made, know that He welcomes you to draw near no matter what you're going through. God adores you, in fact. Today, think of ways you can convey that love to the people in your world. Make their world delightful, fun. Go out of your way to liven their days. In doing so, you will be showing them the love of the Father.

Lord, I delight myself in You! Now show me how to love others
in a way that brings delight to them as well. Amen.

155

Playing

*There is nothing better for a person than that he should
eat and drink and find enjoyment in his toil.
This also, I saw, is from the hand of God.*
ECCLESIASTES 2:24 ESV

You enjoyed them as a child, games like hopscotch, red rover,
hide-and-seek, and dozens of other family-friendly options.
Now, as an adult, you still enjoy the gift of play. In fact, you
activate it when the little ones come around and even when
your elderly friends stop by for a game of cards or dominoes.
Play is an important part of life, no matter your age. It releases
tension, lifts spirits, and reminds you that age is just a number.
Best of all, it's a lovely activity that draws you close to those
you love. (Unless you're a sore loser, of course.) Today, take the
time to think through your play-life. Whom do you play with?
What fond memories are you making? Stay young by staying
active. Activate your play-life!

*I'm still playful at heart, Lord, and I know that trait
comes from You. Thank You for the gift of play
and for those who love to join in the fun. Amen.*

156

Sunshine

*As soon as they come out in leaf, you see for yourselves
and know that the summer is already near.*
LUKE 21:30 ESV

The soft warmth of the summer sun on your face. The golden rays glistening down on the sparkling waters of the ocean. The reflection of the setting sun on a mountaintop. There's just something about sunlight that makes all things right with the world. A warm, sunny day can lift your spirits and make you forget about your troubles. It reminds you that life goes on, that the gray shadows of yesterday have lifted, never to be seen again. Best of all, it illuminates your path so that you can walk freely, unhindered, basking in the glow from heaven above. Today, as you think about the sunlight, ask the Lord how you can be a light for others, a reflection of Him, that they might walk with unhindered steps as well.

*Lord, I'm so grateful for sunny days. They can lift my mood
even when I'm facing obstacles at every turn. Thank You for
that shimmering golden ball in the sky overhead. It's truly one
of your finest creations, one that lights my path. May I be a
shining light to guide the way for others, I pray. Amen.*

157

Calm

The LORD is my shepherd, I lack nothing. He makes me lie down in green pastures, he leads me beside quiet waters, he refreshes my soul. He guides me along the right paths for his name's sake.
PSALM 23:1–3 NIV

You witness it in the peaceful waters of a quiet stream, a calmness that quiets and soothes the soul. You find it in the tranquil face of an elderly woman, content to sit with her thoughts in a rocking chair on the front porch as the hummingbirds light down on the feeder. You observe it in nature as the birds build intricate nests to house their young. Calm. Serene. Peaceful. Tranquil. Relaxed. All of nature gets in on the act, and so can you as you give your cares over to the Lord. He stands ready to swap out your troubles with the kind of peace only He can offer. It soothes, comforts, quiets. It drives away fear, replacing it with blessed assurance. Aren't you grateful for the gift of calm?

Lord, I'm so grateful You take the time to calm my spirit. I don't have to get worked up in a frenzy when things go wrong. You supernaturally intervene, offering the kind of peace that transcends my troubles. I can sit on the porch and relax while You handle things, Lord. I'm so grateful. Amen.

158

Sense of Humor

A joyful heart is good medicine,
but a crushed spirit dries up the bones.
PROVERBS 17:22 ESV

Don't you love folks with a sense of humor? Their timing is impeccable. They can have you belly laughing at the very moment you need a boost. These wonderful, gifted people always see the best in every situation, which means they're fun to hang around. More than anything, they have the uncanny ability to know what tickles your funny bone. They strike like well-aimed darts, always hitting the target and stirring up much-needed laughter, which is—as the Word says—its own medicine. Today, pause to thank the Lord for the gift of laughter. Ask Him to bless those who have this gift so that they can go on blessing others.

Father, I love to laugh. It provides such a beautiful release
and helps me let go of the tensions of the day. May I be one
who tickles the funny bone, Lord, always uplifting
and blessing others with this God-given gift. Amen.

159

Spontaneity

*Preach the word; be ready in season and
out of season; reprove, rebuke, and exhort,
with complete patience and teaching.*
2 TIMOTHY 4:2 ESV

Spontaneous people are so fun. Sure, they leave you biting your
nails at times, but there's something to be said for their fearless
approach to life. Nothing hinders them from plowing ahead,
no matter the obstacles. Spontaneous day trip? No problem!
Quick birthday party for a friend? Sure! Apply for a new job?
Why not? Jet off on a missions trip? Naturally! These impulsive
types love to live on the edge. And while you might not want to
emulate every spontaneous move they make, there's something
to be said for not being held back. Spontaneity can be a gift,
one that gives at a Ping-Pong ball pace.

*Lord, sometimes I'm a little too "in the box." I need to be more
spontaneous. Other times I'm too spontaneous and need to be
reeled in. Show me how to have balance, Father, that my
time on this earth will be well lived for You. Amen.*

160

Curiosity

It is the glory of God to conceal things, but the glory of kings is to search things out. As the heavens for height, and the earth for depth, so the heart of kings is unsearchable.
PROVERBS 25:2–3 ESV

That new kitten is so much fun. She's a curious little thing, peeking under the coffee table, finding cobwebs in the corner, and pouncing on the coffeemaker as if it's some sort of enemy. Her curiosity gets her into trouble some of the time, but mostly it takes her to places she would never have gone before. The same is true with you. If you let your God-given curiosity lead the way, you'll wind up experiencing life with an excitement you never could have predicted. Curiosity is a gift, you see, one meant to pull you out of any ho-humness you might be facing. So look around you. What draws your interest? Let your curiosity take you to places you've never seen before. What an adventure, this gift of curiosity!

Lord, thank You for the gift of curiosity. Life would be dull without it! I'm so glad You've placed me in a world filled with little adventures at every turn. Today I praise You for places I've not yet gone. Take me there, Father. Amen.

161

Playtime

*Also that everyone should eat and drink and take
pleasure in all his toil—this is God's gift to man.*
ECCLESIASTES 3:13 ESV

If someone asked, "What was your favorite class in elementary
school?" likely you would answer, "Recess!" There was something so special about heading out to the playground with your
friends. Whether you played kickball, swung on rusty swings,
or hung upside down from the jungle gym, playtime was the
best. There, in that vast, open space, you could run and play,
casting all academic cares aside. Very little has changed since
then. Sure, you might have aged a little, but playtime is still
great fun. Drinking coffee with your friends. Playing games
with the grandkids. Coloring pictures with your elderly parent.
Sing-alongs with the family on holidays. These special times
draw us closer together and remind us that life isn't all about
work. The Lord created us to play, so join in the game. What fun!

*Father, I'm so glad life isn't all about work. Sometimes I
just need to kick back and enjoy myself. Thank You for the
reminder that playtime—whether it's with friends, loved ones,
or by myself—is a gift, one I'm very grateful for! Amen.*

162

Summer

*"From the fig tree learn its lesson: as soon as its
branch becomes tender and puts out its leaves,
you know that summer is near."*
MARK 13:28 ESV

Voices raised in glee as children splash in the swimming pool.
Glasses of lemonade on the table next to the rocker. Umbrellas
to block the summer sun. Lightweight clothing to keep you
cool. These are all images of summer. No matter what part of
the country you live in, those first few glorious days of summer
bring back terrific memories of childhood, of picnics in the
park, summer sandals, shorts, and T-shirts. Of freedom from
schoolwork, lazy days in the sun, and homemade ice cream.
Summer is a gift. A vacation. A siesta. A reminder that there's
more to life than work. It's freedom to run barefoot, to blow
bubbles, and play tag. This year, as the days heat up, thank the
Lord for the gift of summertime, where the living really is easy.

*Lord, thank You for the summer! I love to watch little ones at
play without a care in the world. I'm so grateful for seasons
that remind me of my childhood, as summer does.
What a blissful time of year, Father. Amen.*

163
Uncontrolled Laughter (Belly Laughs)

He will yet fill your mouth with laughter,
and your lips with shouting.
JOB 8:21 ESV

There's laughter, and then there's belly laughter. It's that over-the-top, whole-body-involved laugh that comes from such a deep place that it almost hurts when you release it. You don't experience it often, but when you do. . .watch out! (If you're shaped like Santa Claus, your "bowl full of jelly" just might jiggle!) Belly laughs have a way of stirring up even more laughter. Before you know it, everyone in the place will be tickled. So don't hold back. Don't get intimidated by others. Who cares if they think you're silly? Just pull the release valve and let the laughter flow. There! Doesn't that feel better?

Lord, I love to laugh. It's such an amazing gift. It makes me
feel better about so many things in my life. May I not be
intimidated by others, Father. Give me the freedom to express
myself through laughter, the best medicine of all. Amen.

164

Sleeping In

*And he said to them, "Come away by yourselves
to a desolate place and rest a while." For many were
coming and going, and they had no leisure even to eat.*
MARK 6:31 ESV

There's no alarm to set. No special plans that require early rising.
You have the morning to sleep in...and you're loving it. On this
special day, you are a woman of leisure, one who won't be ruled
by the clock. You lie in the comfort of your bed until slivers of
sunlight finally rouse you. Instead of bounding from under the
covers, you lie perfectly still, drinking in the half-awakeness. A
song of praise floods your soul, and you wonder where it came
from. Are you still asleep or fully awake now? You yawn and
stretch, cozy and warm, eager for a few more moments before
the stillness is shattered. A few words with your heavenly Father and you're finally ready to swing your legs over the edge
of the bed and face the day. Don't you love sleeping in? What
a restful, glorious gift!

*Thank You for lazy mornings when I can sleep in, Father.
Some days I just need the extra rest. Most of all, I love the
quiet of the morning when You speak so beautifully to my
spirit. What a gift, this precious time with You. Amen.*

Gardens

Why worry about clothes? Look how the wild flowers
grow. They don't work hard to make their clothes.
But I tell you that Solomon with all his wealth
wasn't as well clothed as one of them.
MATTHEW 6:28–29 CEV

She has a green thumb, and she's the envy of everyone in the neighborhood. Each spring her flower gardens bloom with abandon. The colors take your breath away. You see her in the yard, working, working, working to ensure their success. She plants, she waters, she fertilizes, and then, when the moment is right, those first colorful buds peek through. It's no wonder her garden looks terrific while yours barely hangs on. No wonder the "garden of the month" club loves her. She works hard. She's a gardener at heart. Her green thumb gives her an advantage, sure, but so does her tenacity. She's in the yard every chance she can get, and the payoff is terrific. What a gift she is to the community. Her yard brings such joy to all who pass by. What about you? Where do you stand on gardening?

. . . .

Father, I'll admit I'm not the best when it comes to gardening.
My thumb isn't as green as it could be. But I love watching as
others prep their gardens for my enjoyment. The colors
of summer are even better when I'm not the one
doing the work. Bless them, I pray. Amen.

Food

*Behold, what I have seen to be good and fitting is to eat
and drink and find enjoyment in all the toil with which
one toils under the sun the few days of his life
that God has given him, for this is his lot.*
ECCLESIASTES 5:18 ESV

You loved it from the moment Mama first stuck the baby spoon in your mouth. Food, glorious food! And what a variety—the dishes you ate as a child still bring back tasty memories. Those foods you've developed an acquired taste for as an adult are now favorites too. All sorts of yummy delights bring you pleasure. You're a lover of food whether salty, sticky, meaty, or sweet. You love it at home on the supper table or in a restaurant, prepared by others' hands. You love it at the fast-food drive-through, and you love it when a friend invites you over for lunch. Food is a delightful gift, one God meant for us to enjoy. Think of the colors, the varieties, the textures. The Lord has a sense of humor. The same God who created dragon fruit also made the purple eggplant. What an imagination He has! And how He loves for you to use your imagination when you cook and serve those tasty meals.

*God, thank You for the variety of foods I get to enjoy.
You're such a creative, thoughtful Father. May I be just as
creative as I prepare those foods for the ones I love. Amen.*

Safety First

Preach the word; be ready in season and
out of season; reprove, rebuke, and exhort,
with complete patience and teaching.
2 TIMOTHY 4:2 ESV

You're ready to take a trip, and you've prepared for anything that could go wrong: You've had an oil change, checked the spark plugs, filled the tires with air, double-checked your roadside assistance service, checked the spare tire and tire iron. If anything goes wrong, you're ready. Or maybe a storm is coming. You've checked the weather multiple times and know exactly when it's due to land. No worries. You're ready for it. You've filled your pantry, collected bottled water, charged your phone, and filled your tank with gas. You've brought the pets inside, double-checked the outdoor furniture to ensure its safety, and have the number for the electric company handy. No matter what happens, you have a plan. People who have a "safety first" attitude are a real gift (especially to those forgetful types who don't share the same gift). Today, while thanking God for these special people, why not put together a safety plan of your own? Check the smoke alarms, fire extinguisher, batteries, and so on. One day it might come in handy!

Thanks for the reminder, Lord, that safety matters.
Guard and protect us no matter what we face, I pray. Amen.

168

GPS

I will instruct you and teach you in the way you should go;
I will counsel you with my eye upon you.
PSALM 32:8 ESV

━━━━━

"Turn right here. Turn left there. Go 3.2 miles. Your destination *is just ahead on the right.*" You can hear her voice in your head. The GPS lady. You've never met in person, but she's your guide, leading here, there, and everywhere. That time you found yourself in the middle of nowhere, she got you back home again. The time you were invited to a party in a neighborhood you'd never been in? She led you straight to the door. Across the planet, people depend on GPS to get them where they're going. This service is a gift, one that our parents and grandparents didn't have. (Remember maps? Your father opened them and traced a path with his fingertip.) These days, we have the comfort of knowing for sure where we're going. There's safety in knowing we'll arrive at our destination with comfort and ease.

• •

Thank You, Lord, for GPS. I remember what life was like before it. Stopping to make a phone call. Fishing through emails for written directions. These days, that's a thing of the past. Getting from one place to another is easy-breezy, and I'm so grateful. Thank You for directing me, Lord. Amen.

169

Grandparents

Grandchildren are the crown of the aged,
and the glory of children is their fathers.
PROVERBS 17:6 ESV

They show up at the door with gifts for the kids, take them on
fun outings, spend hours playing as if they were kids themselves. Grandparents are a gift. They delight the little ones
with funny stories, jokes, and yummy baked goods. Of course,
they sometimes let those kids get away with more than you got
away with as a child, but you're not complaining. They pour
themselves out for your babies, and you love it. The heart of a
grandparent is resolute. Nothing will ever hurt their grandchild.
Not while they're on watch. You marvel at their passion and
strength and hope (and pray) you'll one day be just like them.
What an amazing gift they are!

Father, I'm grateful for the grandparents I had growing up
and thrilled for the ones I know now. Bless them all, Lord.
Give them good health, energy, and strength for the road
ahead. Most of all, give them an extra dose of childlikeness
so they can keep up with all of those kiddos. Amen.

170

Beaches

That same day Jesus went out of the
house and sat beside the sea.
MATTHEW 13:1 ESV

The breeze blows over the pristine sand in playful fashion, whipping it up and sending it farther down the beach. You walk along the water's edge, pausing only to dip your toes in the water, and then you watch in wide-eyed wonder as the current pulls the waves back out to sea. Your gaze shifts upward to the seagulls overhead, their cawing both mesmerizing and annoying. A deep breath introduces the taste of salt on your lips, and the sand and salt sting your eyes. You love it here. There's something so exquisite about the beach. You feel free, uninhibited. Life is filled with endless possibilities stretching out before you like waves against the shore. Oh, if only you could stand in this carefree place forever. What a gift, this beautiful beach.

Lord, I'm so grateful for beautiful beaches. They take my
breath away! The white sand, blue water, rolling waves. . .
I love it all. I praise You for creating such an amazing
place for me to enjoy. Praise You, Father. Amen.

Swimming Pools

*A messenger you can trust is just as
refreshing as cool water in summer.*
PROVERBS 25:13 CEV

Ah, the local swimming pool! It's filled side-to-side in the summertime with laughing, frolicking, playful kids. Parents hover near the edge, doing their best to keep a close eye on little ones while visiting with one another. The hot days of summer are made cooler by a quick dip in the pool, when you can catch a spot that's not overrun with the kiddos. Whether you have a pool in your backyard or you're forced to swim with hundreds of others at a city pool, there's something to be said for diving in. Cool water. Hot day. It just makes sense. Head for the water and cool down. So what are you waiting for? Grab that suit and get going!

*Father, thank You for cool water on a hot day. Some of my
favorite childhood memories involve swimming pools. I enjoy
the camaraderie, and I also love the physical act of cooling
down in that refreshing water. I love summers, Lord! Amen.*

172

Long Drives

*The LORD will keep your going out and your coming
in from this time forth and forevermore.*
PSALM 121:8 ESV

Long, leisurely drives can be great fun, especially if you're tagging along with someone you adore. Maybe you're taking a drive out to the lake to spend a few quiet hours of reflection. Maybe you're taking the kids to see their grandparents a couple states over. Perhaps you're headed to a conference where you will soak in God's presence. Regardless of your destination, pause to enjoy the journey. It is a gift, you know. Take time to look at the scenery around you. Sing along with the songs on the radio. Swap funny stories with your traveling companions. Pause for snacks at truck stops. Stop to stretch your legs. Look at maps. Pray for God's safety as you travel. Then have fun every step of the way.

*Father, I'm reminded of the road trips I took as a youngster.
What fun we had, mile after crazy mile. Thank You for
keeping us safe those many, many times. And thank You for
the joy of traveling with others. What a gift, Lord! Amen.*

Playgrounds

And the streets of the city shall be full of boys
and girls playing in its streets.
ZECHARIAH 8:5 ESV

Swings. Slides. Jungle gyms. Kids. Parents. Grandparents. Sweaty clothes. Juice boxes. Squeals of delight. These are all images of time spent on the playground with the kids. Running to and fro, chasing one another, playing hide-and-seek. . .who can resist when the play area makes it all so appealing? These special places, specifically designed for play, are a real gift for families. They provide a safe environment to spend time together. When was the last time you went to a playground with the kids or grandkids? Maybe it's been too long. Why not put together a picnic lunch and head out for some fun in the sun?

Lord, I love those special play areas for the kids. They make
me feel young again. It's so great to watch the children at
play, so carefree, so social. I have so much to learn from
them as they gather with other youngsters for this
joyous time together. May I never forget
the value of playing, Father. Amen.

Childlike Joy

*And they offered great sacrifices that day
and rejoiced, for God had made them rejoice with
great joy; the women and children also rejoiced.*
NEHEMIAH 12:43 ESV

Some people have that simple childlike joy, no matter their age. Their eyes reflect wonder at God's creation. They laugh at silly jokes and enjoy life to the fullest as a child would. They don't hold grudges or anger easily. These innocent ones are so full of life, so happy to be alive, that their joy spills over onto others. You love hanging around people like this because of their contagious zeal for life. You want in on the action. So you watch how they interact with others, how they respond when things go wrong. You note that childlike joy stems from a deep place of trusting the Lord, and you commit to that same sort of relationship with your heavenly Father.

*Father, I love the innocence of children. I also love it when
one of my adult friends has that same wide-eyed wonder,
Lord. These sweet, joyful people are so fun to be around.
Show me how to live like that, I pray. Amen.*

175

Hugs

*And he arose and came to his father. But while he was
still a long way off, his father saw him and felt compassion,
and ran and embraced him and kissed him.*
LUKE 15:20 ESV

They come just when you need them. They surround you,
press in close, and whisper, "Peace, be still." Hugs are a tangible reminder of God's presence. He uses the arms of a friend,
a loved one, a parent, a child, to intervene, to say, "I'm right
here. You're not alone." Hugs say, "Hey! Haven't seen you in a
while!" or "You are worthy of love and affection." Of course, hugs
don't come naturally to everyone. In fact, you might be a non-
hugger. Today, let your guard down. Embrace (pun intended)
the notion that hugs are a gift. They're meant to show you that
you are loved. They're also a gift you can give others. If you
have a friend who's hurting, she might need the reassurance
that only a hug can bring. So what's keeping you? Open your
arms wide. . .and embrace the possibilities!

*Thank You for the reminder, Lord, that some people just need
a good hug. May I be that person who stops and embraces
those in pain. And may I be willing to accept an embrace
even when I feel like pushing others away.
Soften my heart, I pray. Amen.*

176

Innocence

But when Jesus saw it, he was indignant and said to them, "Let the children come to me; do not hinder them, for to such belongs the kingdom of God."
MARK 10:14 ESV

~

Don't you love the innocence of a child? So trusting. So precious. So pure. That's exactly how God calls us to live, no matter our age. He wants us to trust with such devotion as a little one would trust a mother or father. He wants us to live with such purity of heart, mind, and body that no one will question our motives or actions. He longs for us to stare up at Him as a toddler would gaze at her papa, wide-eyed with love and admiration for Daddy-God. How long has it been since you entered God's presence with the innocence and wonder of a little girl? Perhaps it's time to do so now. Rush into His arms, tell Him your troubles, and watch as He kisses away your tears and makes all things new again.

* * *

Oh Father, I come to You today as a wide-eyed child, in awe of Your presence. I trust You, Daddy-God, to care for me, Your daughter, with tenderness and love. Restore my innocence, I pray, and renew my passion for purity of heart, mind, and body. Amen.

Listening

He who has ears to hear, let him hear.
MATTHEW 11:15 ESV

Shh. Can you hear it? Lean in close. She's laughing. He's coughing. Horns are honking. Utensils are scraping against plates. Shoes are clacking across floors. All around you, noises abound. Every minute of every day, there's something to be heard even if it's just the sound of your heart beating in your chest. Are you a listener? Do you home in on what's going on around you? Listening is a gift particularly when it comes to listening closely as a friend shares her heart. Are you paying attention, or are you distracted by incoming text messages? Do you really hear what she's saying, or have you checked out? Today, make up your mind to be a good listener. Give your friends and loved ones the gift of your undivided attention when they speak. You might just need that gift returned to you at some point in the future, so listen up!

Lord, I want to be a good listener, but so often my thoughts stray. I'm there in body but not in spirit. I've already checked out. Today, tune my ears to hear—to really hear—what others are saying. I want to offer the gift of listening to all who need an ear, Father. Help me, I pray. Amen.

178

Good Books

*As for these four youths, God gave them learning
and skill in all literature and wisdom, and Daniel
had understanding in all visions and dreams.*
DANIEL 1:17 ESV

They beg for you to open them. Their stories keep you awake at night. They line your shelves and spill over onto the end tables. Many gather dust, and others have worn, dog-eared pages and sections highlighted in yellow. Books are so much a part of you that you couldn't do without them. Between their colorful covers, you are swept away to simpler times, transported to other parts of the country, and lifted out of your doldrums. You learn countless life lessons, discover new truths, and determine to be the best you that you can be. Books are a gift, one you treasure. You give them as presents and accept them with joy. They will continue to be a part of your life for as long as you live, and you're grateful for them.

*I'm a book lover, Lord! (Of course, You already knew that.)
I can't wait to get my hands on a good story or a fabulous
nonfiction book. I've learned so much about who I am through
the pages. Thank You for giving authors the words to
pen, Father. As a reader, I'm so grateful. Amen.*

179

Electricity

"For nothing will be impossible with God."
LUKE 1:37 ESV

❧

It lights your home, heats your stove, washes and dries your clothes. It cools the air around you, gives the microwave its power, and ensures hot coffee in the morning. Electricity is so much a part of your everyday life that you barely pay it any mind. . .until it goes out. During those hours, as the house sits dark and quiet, you realize your dependence on your power source. Things just aren't the same without it. Life moves at a completely different pace. You can't charge your phone or reading device. You've lost the use of your computer, your internet. Everything grinds to a halt. And then—whew!—the lights pop back on. All's right with the world. Aren't you glad you live in the modern age where electricity is an option? What are you waiting for? Heat that stove! Bake those cookies. Make that coffee. Fully enjoy the gift of electricity.

I'm so grateful to live in the modern age, Lord. You power my life with this amazing gift. Things wouldn't be the same without it. Thanks for lighting my world, Father! Amen.

180

Silliness

He will yet fill your mouth with laughter,
and your lips with shouting.
JOB 8:21 ESV

Oh, the antics of childhood! Tickling the tummy, chasing a younger sibling through the house, stacking blocks, telling jokes. You giggled, you laughed, you had the time of your life. And then you grew up. Perhaps the silly, giggly part of you remained behind in childhood. It's time to dust off the tickle monster and bring her out to play. Just because you're an adult doesn't mean you can't be silly. God loves for His kids to have fun. So gather your friends together. Laugh. Play games. Tell funny stories that make you chuckle. Share your joys. Don't worry about what others will think about you during these moments of silliness. Just be yourself, and enjoy the gift of carefree, childlike abandon.

Father, I love to be silly. Laughter is so good for my soul.
I'm reminded of my time as a child, when I'd have such a
good time with friends and siblings. I want that same
carefree living now, Lord. Show me how to release
my cares and simply enjoy life! Amen.

Snacks

How sweet are your words to my taste,
sweeter than honey to my mouth!
PSALM 119:103 ESV

It's the little between-meal snack that keeps you going when your tummy grumbles. A protein bar, a handful of nuts, a piece of chocolate—that little treat says, "You can make it until dinnertime. Don't give up!" It's the ice-cream bar, the slice of cheese, the candy bar, the half slice of pizza. It gets you over the hump so you can get more work done. Aren't you grateful for these mini-meals, these yummy snacks? They break up your day and give you something to look forward to. They're a blessing, just the right thing to rouse you when midafternoon grogginess kicks in. Snacks are a yummy-in-the-tummy gift.

Lord, I love to snack. I'm so grateful for those mini-
meals. They're a lot of fun and give me something to look
forward to when the day is getting long. Help me to
not overindulge, Father, but only to take what
I need. I praise You for special treats. Amen.

182

Adventure

So, whether you eat or drink, or whatever you do,
do all to the glory of God.
1 CORINTHIANS 10:31 ESV

They get your heart pounding in anticipation and keep you excited about what's coming next. Life's little adventures are a gift. Whether it's a quick trip to the river to go tubing or a long-awaited visit to a theme park, you have adventures a-plenty in mind for your crew, and you can't wait. You plan. You save. You prepare. And then you wait until the perfect moment to spring the big plan on everyone. Joy radiates throughout your home as the news is absorbed. Before long, everyone is packing for the big adventure. So where are you headed next? Why not take the time to plan your next big adventure? Don't be afraid to dream big!

Lord, I love planning little adventures. These trips, these
journeys, are so much fun. I know that the grandest
adventure of all is the one You've planned for me,
Father—a life spent with You followed by eternity
in the grandest adventure of all. I can
hardly wait, Lord. Amen.

Dealing Fairly with Others

*"Now swear to me here before God that you will not
deal falsely with me or my children or my descendants.
Show to me and the country where you now reside as
a foreigner the same kindness I have shown to you."*
GENESIS 21:23 NIV

People can be so wonderful, stepping in to help you when you
find yourself in a jam. But there are also those people who want
to take advantage of others, to do all they can to milk situations
or make a buck. They're skilled manipulators, many of them.
That's why it's so refreshing to find people who deal truthfully
with others. When you find someone like that (say, a mechanic
or a doctor who cuts you some slack because you don't have
insurance), you've found a friend for life. These fine folks aren't
out to snag every dollar they can from you. Rather, they put
the needs of others above their own and always with a broad
smile. Today, think back to the many times you were dealt with
fairly, and then commit to offer that same kindness to others.

*Lord, thank You for those wonderful businesspeople who
deal fairly with others. I'm so grateful for their kindness.
Show me how I can reach out to others with that same
love, Father, that all might sense Your goodness. Amen.*

184

Friendliness

*And let us consider how to stir up one another to love
and good works, not neglecting to meet together,
as is the habit of some, but encouraging one another,
and all the more as you see the Day drawing near.*
HEBREWS 10:24–25 ESV

You see him every time you pull the car out of the driveway.
He's that one neighbor who's always out and about, watering
his yard, visiting with a neighbor, fixing a friend's broken fence
post, waving at others as they pass by. He's a friendly guy and
helpful as well. If a single mom needs her oil changed, he's
there. A kid in the neighborhood loses a ball, he finds it. A
dog goes missing, he's on the hunt to find him. This fella is
naturally good-natured and known among the neighbors as a
Good Samaritan. And you're drawn to him too. In fact, you'd
like to be more like him—drawn to others, ready to wave at
neighbors passing by. What a precious gift friendly folks are!

*Lord, thank You for making some people extra-friendly.
There are days when people need a smile, a wave,
a handshake. These folks are ready to roll.
What a blessing they are, Father. Amen.*

Water

*"Whoever believes in me, as the Scripture has said,
'Out of his heart will flow rivers of living water.'"*
JOHN 7:38 ESV

Across this great big world people fight to find water to drink.
Many walk for miles each day just for a tiny cup of water. It's
hard to fathom in this day and age, but people are literally
dying of thirst. Most likely, you live in an area where water is
found in abundance. You have plenty to drink and even more
for things like laundry and bathing. It never enters your mind
that your proverbial well might run dry. Today, thank God
for the gift of abundant water, and then do some perusing on
the web to find an organization building wells in third-world
countries. Maybe God is nudging you to play a role in bringing
water to someone else.

*Father, thank You for that nudge. I'm grateful for the
abundance of water in my neck of the woods, but I'm keenly
aware that other people only have it in short supply.
How can I help, Lord? Show me, that I might get
involved. Bless You for this nudge. Amen.*

186

Independence

Now the Lord is the Spirit, and where the
Spirit of the Lord is, there is freedom.
2 CORINTHIANS 3:17 ESV

~

Banners. Streamers. Fireworks. Picnics. People cheering. Voices raised as neighbors come together. These are images of the Fourth of July. Independence Day is celebrated across the nation, a reminder that we are no longer bound to another country. We are our own. Bought and paid for at a great, terrible price. The same is true in your own life. Christ died to set you free, that you would not be bound to sin. You are His now, free from bondage. He paid the ultimate price and would do it again out of love for you. Today, as you contemplate the freedom of a nation, think of the freedom Christ has placed in your heart. Where will you go from here now that you are free? Only He knows, but it will be an amazing journey!

Father, thank You for independence. I'm so glad to be walking
in freedom. Chains are broken. Scales have fallen from
my eyes. I'm yours, Lord, and I'm free! Amen.

187

Reflections

For now we see in a mirror dimly, but then face to face.
Now I know in part; then I shall know fully,
even as I have been fully known.
1 CORINTHIANS 13:12 ESV

You walk by the mirror and give yourself a second glance. Your hair is a bit messy, and you need to touch up your lipstick. You turn sideways and gaze at your profile. Sucking in your stomach, you look again. Frustrated, you release your breath and go back to your natural position. It's true, you don't always like what you see in the mirror. Your reflection doesn't lie. Every freckle, every wrinkle, every flaw is evident at a glance. But think about what your life would be like without the ability to see your reflection. You would be so limited—no way to check your hairdo, your makeup, your hemline. No sense of whether or not your blouse and skirt went together or your jewelry looked okay with that ensemble. Mirrors might show us every bump and wrinkle, but they're still a blessing, one we wouldn't want to live without.

Lord, I don't always like the reflection staring back at me,
but I'm still grateful for mirrors. Thank You for giving
us the option to see what needs to be seen so
we can do what needs to be done. Amen.

188

Patriotism

*And there you shall eat before the LORD your God,
and you shall rejoice, you and your households, in all that
you undertake, in which the LORD your God has blessed you.*
DEUTERONOMY 12:7 ESV

～

You love this country. It's a part of your fiber, your being. When the flag waves in front of you, your heart wants to burst with pride. When the national anthem is sung, tears come to your eyes. You're forever linked to this great nation, and nothing will ever change that. The way you feel about it—those feelings of patriotism and pride—they're a gift. They say, "You can't take this away from me. No matter what else happens in my life, I'm still linked to a land, a people, a nation." What an amazing feeling to be part of something so grand, so glorious, so all-encompassing.

*Father, how I love this country! I love the freedoms I have,
the feelings of neighborliness from those around me, and the
sense of pride we share as we celebrate our freedoms together.
I'm so grateful for those who defend my freedom and risk
their lives that I might live in peace. Thank You for those
freedoms, Lord. May I never take them for granted. Amen.*

189

Celebrations

*" 'And bring the fattened calf and kill it, and let us eat
and celebrate. For this my son was dead, and is alive again;
he was lost, and is found.' And they began to celebrate."*
LUKE 15:23-24 ESV

$\sim$

You plan for weeks. The guest list is made. You purchase decorations, arrange for food items, bake a cake, cookies, or cupcakes. Finally, the moment arrives. That birthday, wedding, baby shower, holiday celebration is finally here, and you're thrilled! Perhaps you're the sort who loves hosting events like this. Maybe you excel at decorating. You could put together a themed bridal shower in your sleep. You've done so many Valentine's banquets, it's not a chore for you. You just love celebrations. Or maybe you're the sort to hover in the background while someone else does the planning. Regardless, gatherings like this are so much fun. They're the perfect opportunity to see folks you don't get to see every day and to have a few hours of childlike celebration!

*Lord, thank You for those who have the gift of hospitality,
the ones who are so good at whipping together a big party.
The creative juices are flowing at many of these events.
Bless those with a spirit of hospitality, I pray. Amen.*

190

A Smile

A glad heart makes a cheerful face, but by sorrow of heart the spirit is crushed. The heart of him who has understanding seeks knowledge, but the mouths of fools feed on folly.
PROVERBS 15:13-14 ESV

She doesn't offer you much. It doesn't cost her a penny. But she flashes that smile, and your whole world changes. In that instant, you forget about the angst with the kids. You let go of the frustration about finances. You forgive your boss for speaking to you like a child. Her smile changes everything. And she doesn't even know what you're going through. She's just being friendly. You know though, and you recognize God's timing. So you pass by the next person and you smile not just because it's a friendly thing to do but because you just never know what she might be going through.

Father, my life has been turned around by a simple smile from a stranger or coworker. It's happened more times than I can count. You send these people at just the right time, offering just the right incentive to release my woes. That smile literally turns my frown upside down. And it's contagious! Thank You, Lord. Amen.

191

Birds Chirping

Beside them the birds of the heavens dwell;
they sing among the branches.
PSALM 104:12 ESV

They're outside your window, singing their midmorning song. You peer out to see they've gathered on the bird feeder. Their lovely trill fills the air as they nibble, nibble, nibble on food then clean themselves. You love to watch them at play as they light on the fence and then rise into the air once again, but you're even more mesmerized by their songs. Who gives them the melody? How do they know when to sing and when to quit? You sense the Lord's hand at work in their lives just as He works in yours. Your midmorning song is pretty amazing too. Sure, you're just humming a worship chorus, but to God it's an orchestrated masterpiece, a heart lifted in praise to Him.

Lord, thank You for the reminder that all of creation lifts a
song to you. I love listening to the birds who grace me with
their presence. I also love to lift a song of praise to You,
Father. May it bless Your heart just as these little ones
bless mine. All praise to You, Lord! Amen.

Picnics

Think about my words, as you would taste food.
JOB 34:3 CEV

The quilt has been spread on the prettiest patch of grass you could find. The basket's open, revealing the goodies inside: sandwiches, chips, fruit, veggies, and bottled water. You reach for the paper plates and napkins, ready to get this show on the road. You call out to the children, "Come and get it!" and they come running. Minutes later, surrounded by those you love, you're enjoying the finest meal you've shared in ages. There's something so special about a picnic. It makes the ordinary (sandwiches and chips) seem extraordinary. Seated on the ground, legs crossed, you feel carefree and young again. Something about this outdoor experience whisks you back in time, and you're a child, running across the park, straight to your mother's quilt, so that you can nibble on peanut butter sandwiches and swap stories to make her laugh. Oh, the joy of a picnic. Maybe it's time to host one. Whom can you invite?

Lord, I love feeling carefree. I don't have to go outdoors to get that feeling, but it doesn't hurt. Show me how to create experiences for those I love—children, grandchildren, and so on. I want to instill memories they will never forget. Help me with creative ideas, Father. Amen.

193

Movies

*Work the first six days of the week, but rest and relax on the
seventh day. This law is not only for you, but for your oxen,
donkeys, and slaves, as well as for any foreigners among you.*
EXODUS 23:12 CEV

⁓

They sweep you away to happier times, to dramas unfolding,
to emotions you didn't know you possessed. There, in the quiet
darkness of the theater or the stillness of your living room,
you're transported, lifted out of your everydayness and placed
smack-dab in someone else's story. You don't have to contribute
to the tale; indeed, it is there for your viewing pleasure. So you
sit and watch, happy to have the freedom to observe. These
moments, when you're caught up in a good movie, are blissful.
There are no problems to solve, no dishes to wash, no laundry
to fold. For approximately two hours, you have the freedom to
just. . .be. What a lovely gift.

*Father, I enjoy watching other people's stories. They entertain.
They educate. They lift my spirits. I don't slip away into the
world of make-believe often, but when I do, it's such a sweet
escape. I'm grateful for good storytellers, Lord. Amen.*

194

Transportation

For he will command his angels concerning
you to guard you in all your ways.
PSALM 91:11 NIV

～

They get you where you need to go—planes, trains, and automobiles. They move at different rates of speed, and you get to choose which one you want to take. No matter which one you choose, your chances of arriving in a timely fashion are good. Compare that to a century ago when automobiles were just coming on the scene. Before that, people traveled by stagecoach, horse and wagon, or possibly on trains as they headed out West to seek their fortunes. You though? You hop into your car, complete with AC and heated seats, and arrive at your destination in no time. Your modern vehicle is a gift, one you likely overlook. Today, take a moment to thank God for modern transportation and for the excitement of traveling to and fro in such speedy fashion.

Lord, thank You for all modes of transportation—subway,
train, car, planes, and boats. I can't even imagine what my
life would be like if I didn't have a way to get around.
I'm grateful, Father, for all the options. Amen.

Living Life Fully

And I heard the voice of the Lord saying, "Whom shall I send, and who will go for us?" Then I said, "Here I am! Send me."
ISAIAH 6:8 ESV

You live life to the fullest. When others are just barely getting by, you're going at it full tilt. Go big or go home. That's your motto. You want to squeeze every bit of juice out of life, to make lemonade out of even the toughest situations. And having this perspective has grown you into a woman of strength. Others come to you for advice. They want to know how to get more out of their lives, how to get past the doldrums, the everyday-ness, the boredom. You share what you've learned, you tell of this gift called "fullness," and others join in, ready to live with abundance as you are doing. Where does it come from, this abundance? From a life centered on Jesus Christ, of course. He did promise to bring life to the fullest, and you're taking full advantage of that.

Lord, I want to live an abundant life even when things aren't going my way. I know this is possible, Father. I submit myself to Your fullness. Fill me. Use me. Then send me to those who need to know more about You, I pray. Amen.

Wind Chimes

He sends his word and melts them;
he stirs up his breezes, and the waters flow.
PSALM 147:18 NIV

They soothe and delight you, their tinkling sound music to your ears. They're a reminder that breezes still blow, peace is possible, and life has a quiet musical sound track to calm your soul when you need it. You love those wind chimes. When gentle winds blow through, they put out the loveliest tinkling sound. When a major storm hits, they sound like an orchestra warming up before the big show. Most of all, their delightful music reminds you that God, the Author of all, cares about even the tiniest things in your life. He knows that you delight in the sound of those chimes and sends little breezes to tickle your ears, to bring pleasure on an otherwise difficult day. What a gift, these special, musical moments!

Father, You're there in the cool, soothing morning breeze,
singing Your song over me. You care about the details
of my life so much that You tend to the finest ones.
I love the sound track You've created, and I'm
so grateful for Your love, Lord. Amen.

Flight

*If I take the wings of the morning and dwell in the
uttermost parts of the sea, even there your hand shall
lead me, and your right hand shall hold me.*
PSALM 139:9-10 ESV

You can be in New York in three hours. Los Angeles, about the
same. No matter where you're traveling, you can get there in
just a few hours' time, and all because of air travel. It's hard to
imagine what life was like for travelers a hundred years ago. If
someone wanted to leave Kansas and drive to California, the
journey would take days. Now a couple of hours will suffice.
The ability to fly back and forth from place to place is a gift,
one we often take for granted. Missionaries fly to the foreign
mission fields. Businessmen make a day trip for the company.
Children fly to see parents in other states and vice versa. The
ease and comfort of air travel makes all this possible. What a
miracle of convenience flight is! How grateful we are to live in
a day and age where this is possible.

*Father, sometimes I forget to be mesmerized by things like
air travel. It seems so commonplace to me, but it's a miracle.
I can get from here to there in no time, thanks to this modern
marvel. Thank You for giving us the gift of flight, Lord. Amen.*

198

Grandchildren

May you see your children's children!
Peace be upon Israel!
PSALM 128:6 ESV

They make your heart sing. His freckled face. Her messy hair. Those lollypop-sticky fingers. Those kids are your grandchildren, and you wouldn't trade them for anything in the world even on the messiest of days. They're your legacy, your heritage, your hopes, your dreams, all wrapped up in sticky little packages. They remind you of your days as a young mom, when your kiddos were young. They also remind you that life goes on from generation to generation. Most of all, you adore spending time with them because they love you with reckless abandon. Whether you're baking cookies, watching a TV show, or playing games, those grandkids can't wait to spend time with their grandparents. What a gift, these precious ones!

Father, thank You for my grandchildren. I adore them, Lord.
They make me feel young again. I'm a child playing with
toys, watching kiddy TV shows, and eating gummy
bears. What fun, to spend time with my favorite
people on the planet. Praise You. Amen.

Noise

Make a joyful noise to the LORD, all the earth;
break forth into joyous song and sing praises!
PSALM 98:4 ESV

Sometimes it drives you crazy—all that noise from the kids, the neighbors, the music playing overhead in restaurants. There's a never-ending sound track, especially when someone turns on the TV while you're trying to have a quiet discussion, or the kids start squabbling when you have a headache. Where would you be without that sound track though? It's a part of you, and it's a gift. Instead of allowing the noise to frustrate you, pause for a moment and drink it in. It's a sign that all is right in your world. Those squabbles? That music? That blaring TV? These are indicators that the people in your world are close by, and you wouldn't change that for anything in the world no matter how noisy!

Father, thank You for reminding me that noise can be a good thing. It's a lovely reminder that those I love are hovering close. Today I thank You for that noise because it's a reflection of the people I adore. Amen.

Little Pleasures

*You make known to me the path of life; in your presence there
is fullness of joy; at your right hand are pleasures forevermore.*
PSALM 16:11 ESV

Life is filled with little pleasures. Lunch at a tearoom with a
friend. Playing with a friend's new puppy. Holding your infant
grandchild for the first time. Fishing with Dad. Picnics with the
cousins. Floating in a raft down the river. Watching a funny
movie with a friend. These "little" pleasures all add up to one
terrific life. And you love those moments, even the ones that
whiz by at the speed of light. They are a gift. In fact, you love
them so much that you've taken to planning them for others.
To bring a smile to a neighbor's face, you leave a little gift at
her front door. For the family in need, you provide gift cards
for a meal out. Everywhere you go, you're making sure others
have the little pleasures you enjoy. . .and it feels mighty good.
Little pleasures are a gift that keeps on giving.

*Father, I love those little, special moments. They mean
so much to me. Show me how to give away little pleasures
to those I love. May they all be blessed as
I've been blessed, Lord. Amen.*

Baby Giggles

He will yet fill your mouth with laughter,
and your lips with shouting.
JOB 8:21 ESV

Oh, that adorable baby! He's just reaching that "I'm getting verbal!" stage, and you can't get enough of him. He giggles and wriggles, those lips curling up in the most delightful smile you've ever witnessed. You tickle him once more just so you can hear it again. He squeals with delight. You squeal in response. As he coos and babbles, you're swept away. Nothing else matters. The bills. The frustrations. The argument you had with your husband. It's all gone for these few, fleeting moments. This baby's joyous offering has erased every woe and reminded you that joy can wipe away pain even if the joy originates in one so tiny he didn't realize you were struggling. What a gift, those baby giggles!

Father, thank You for using the sound of laughter to lift my
spirits. I love this little baby so much, Lord. Those giggles
are a constant reminder of all that's right with the world.
Give me the lightheartedness of this child, I pray. Amen.

202

Paper Plates

*Also that everyone should eat and drink
and take pleasure in all his toil—this is God's gift to man.*
ECCLESIASTES 3:13 ESV

Guests are on their way. Lots of them. You've prepared food. They're bringing more food. You baked a cake and checked the ice-cream supply. The plan? To eat and visit, possibly for hours on end, then eat and visit some more. You reach into the pantry and pull out your best weapon, one that will make this day far more enjoyable—paper plates. Today they are your best friend. They're the gift that keeps on giving. No dishes to wash, no messy food to scrape. Just toss those plates in the trash and spend more time with your loved ones. It's the little conveniences like this that we often take for granted, but they provide us extra moments with those we love. What a gift for the busy family!

Lord, thank You for items like paper plates that make my life so much easier. I could do it the old-fashioned way, but sometimes a girl just needs a break. There are so many little things like this I take for granted, but I'm grateful for every one. Bless You, Lord. Amen.

Citizenship

*But our citizenship is in heaven, and from it we await a Savior,
the Lord Jesus Christ, who will transform our lowly body
to be like his glorious body, by the power that enables
him even to subject all things to himself.*
PHILIPPIANS 3:20–21 ESV

You are a citizen of a state, a country, a planet, but you're also a
citizen of heaven. Might seem strange, since you're not exactly
in heaven yet, but you already have the stamp in your passport.
You received it the day you asked Jesus into your heart. Right
away, heaven was your home—both now and in the future. God
planted the seeds on the day of your rebirth (when you came
alive in Him), and every step you've taken since has moved you
closer and closer to your ultimate home. Once you pass from
this life to the next, you'll feel right at home in heaven because
you're already a citizen. Best of all, you've already spent lots of
time with your Daddy-God. He's had wonderful things for you
in this life. Can you even imagine what He has in store for you
once you arrive in heaven for good?

*Father, I know my citizenship is in heaven. I'm not afraid
to pass from one life to another when my time comes.
I'm looking forward to spending eternity with
You and with those I love, Lord. Amen.*

204

Extended Family

But if anyone does not provide for his relatives,
and especially for members of his household, he has
denied the faith and is worse than an unbeliever.
1 TIMOTHY 5:8 ESV

Large families have the best reunions. Aunts. Uncles. Cousins. More cousins. Still more cousins. Grandparents. Moms. Dads. They line the tables, chowing down on potluck foods each has brought to the party. The kids play with cousins they didn't even remember having, while the grown-ups get caught up on what they've missed since the last reunion. There's something so special about these extended family members. You're linked by blood (or love), and though you don't see each other often, you still feel bonded. Today, as you pause to pray for your loved ones, don't forget these special folks. They're as much a part of you as ever and need your prayer covering.

Lord, I want to thank You for all of my family members,
even the ones I rarely see. Today I lift them all before
Your throne, Father—aunts, uncles, cousins, and so on.
Bless. Heal. Touch. Revive. Keep this family
on fire for You, Father, I pray. Amen.

Modesty

I appeal to you therefore, brothers, by the mercies of God,
to present your bodies as a living sacrifice, holy and
acceptable to God, which is your spiritual worship.
ROMANS 12:1 ESV

Perhaps it's hard to imagine modesty as a gift, but it is. It's that little extra *oomph* that says, "I'm taking my purity seriously. I'm not trying to draw attention to myself; rather, I'm trying to draw attention to Christ." A woman can be modest in dress, modest in speech, and modest in action. God longs for us to be all three. Sure, it's fun to dress in trendy clothes, but you know when those clothes cross a line, when they're no longer cute but "too sexy." You know where to draw the line because you want to honor God in all you do. You also know that the world needs the gift of modesty so guys can stay pure too. So go on. Choose the right clothes. Speak the right words. Live the right life. Your modesty will be a gift, an example, to others you meet along the way.

Father, thank You for the reminder that modesty is a gift.
I want to be known as a woman who's modest in clothing,
speech, and living. May I set an example for
those who follow, Lord. Amen.

Making Memories

*You shall love the L<small>ORD</small> your God with all your heart and with
all your soul and with all your might. And these words that I
command you today shall be on your heart. You shall teach
them diligently to your children, and shall talk of them when
you sit in your house, and when you walk by the way,
and when you lie down, and when you rise.*
D<small>EUTERONOMY</small> 6:5–7 <small>ESV</small>

Opportunities abound. You find them at every turn. Baking
cookies with the grandkids. A quiet dinner with your oldest
daughter. Shopping for that wedding dress with your best
friend. Helping your son and daughter-in-law paint their baby's
bedroom a lovely shade of blue. Life gives you amazing opportunities to make memories with those you love. They don't have
to be breathtaking events, paid for in advance. Memory-making
can happen as you've gathered around the breakfast table or on
a drive to school. Wherever and whenever you're with friends,
family, or loved ones, you have an opportunity to create memories that will last for decades. So what's on the agenda today?
What memories will you create?

*Father, I want to be a memory-maker. I want to provide
opportunities for memories that will last for years to
come. I invite You to be a part of every conversation,
every experience, every meeting. Bind our hearts,
and give us memories that will last, I pray. Amen.*

Legacy

One generation shall commend your works to another,
and shall declare your mighty acts.
PSALM 145:4 ESV

Your grandparents passed it to your father. He, in turn, passed it down to you. Your legacy, that special, inexplicable, sometimes tangible gift left by those who've gone before is unique to you, your family. It's the foods you eat, the church you attend, the way you speak. It's the funny phrases you use, the way you tidy up the kitchen, the kind of clothes you wear. Your legacy is your heritage (what you've inherited), something you're very proud of. You see it as a gift, and that's just what it is. You want to pass it to your children too, so you start early, teaching them the family ways. Generations from now, that amazing legacy will carry on with the hints and flavors of all your family members factored in. How precious, this amazing legacy!

Father, I'm so thrilled to be part of a bigger story. You've been there for my parents, grandparents, and so on, and I know You'll be there for my children. What a legacy my ancestors have passed to me. May I do right by them and share all I can with my children and grandchildren.
Thank You, Father. Amen.

Old Photographs

But Mary treasured up all these things,
pondering them in her heart.
LUKE 2:19 ESV

⁓

You reach for the box of photos and draw in a deep breath. You can almost picture how this is going to go. Looking over old family photos does a number on you. Your emotions roll up and down like a tide being pulled in and out. You look at the pictures one by one, your heart in your throat. The one of your mother as a little girl nearly moves you to tears. What a beautiful little girl. You see some of your daughter in that face. The photo of your father is bittersweet. What you wouldn't give to have just five more minutes with him. By the time you get to the pictures of your children, you're a mess. These old photos have taken you to a place you hadn't planned to go. They are a gift, a reminder of days gone by. How precious, this lovely reminder.

. . . .

Father, thank You for stirring up these memories inside me
as I look at old photos. I don't want to forget. Sure, it's painful
looking at smiling faces of people who've left this life,
but I want to remember them as they were so
I might pass on the stories to my children.
I'm grateful, Lord. Very grateful. Amen.

Family Trees

Take your whole family with you into the boat, because you are the only one on this earth who pleases me.
GENESIS 7:1 CEV

It unfolds before you like a perfectly manicured map of relatives. Your family tree. You start at the top, reading your own name, then travel down to your parents, grandparents, and so on. Before long, hours have passed, and you're still marveling over the many, many people in your family tree. If you're like some folks, you enjoy researching your relatives online. You spend weeks putting together a tree, gathering details like birth and death records, military service, and even photographs. You love this process and can't wait to learn more about those who came before you. They are like old friends, characters in a story, filled with delightful tales. And you love them because their stories are now part of your story too.

Father, I love finding out about my relatives—my grandparents, great-grandparents, and so on. What interesting lives they led, Lord. How different from my own. And yet I am who I have become at least in part because of their sacrifices, their journeys. It's remarkable to think about, Father. I praise You for my family tree. Amen.

Weekends

I know the best thing we can do is to always enjoy life.
ECCLESIASTES 3:12 CEV

∿

Friday afternoon can't come soon enough for you. It's been a long week. You're ready for a break. You've been counting down the hours until the clock strikes five. When it does, you spring from your workplace and head for the car, ready to get this weekend under way. No matter what you have planned—a family outing, dinner and a movie with your best friend, or laundry—you're going to enjoy it. Even the simple act of lounging around on the sofa as the weekend's hours while by sounds good to you. So does spending time at church with your friends. Weekends are a gift because they give us a much-needed break from routine. They help us refocus on what's really important and offer opportunity to rest. No matter what you're up to this weekend, remember. . .it's a gift!

Thank You for the gift of the weekend, Lord. Sometimes I get so weary with day-in, day-out living. Weekends remind me life isn't all about work. It's also about family, faith, and friendship. I plan to share in all three this weekend, Lord. Amen.

Fun Traditions

So then, as we have opportunity, let us do good to everyone,
and especially to those who are of the household of faith.
GALATIANS 6:10 ESV

Your family has lots of fun traditions. The way they open presents on Christmas. The foods they enjoy. The restaurants they frequent. The vacations they take. Many of these came from their parents, and their parents before them. It's fun to pass down favorite foods, phrases, and ways of living. It's also exciting to pass down your family's ethnic culture. Knowing more about where your people come from, those traditions they shared in—back in Scotland, Germany, South Africa, or wherever else they came from—can be such a blast. So do your research. Find out what makes your family tick. Then share those traditions with the next generation so that no one ever forgets.

I love finding out more about my family's traditions, Lord. I
want to know where my people came from, why they ate the
foods they did, spoke the way they did, wore the kinds
of clothes they did. This is all a part of my legacy, and I
can't wait to pass it down to the next generation.
Thanks for stirring me to action. Amen.

Neighborly Affection

To everyone who is thirsty, he gives something to drink;
to everyone who is hungry, he gives good things to eat.
PSALM 107:9 CEV

Don't you love it when the community comes together? Maybe it's a "night out with neighbors" event or a major holiday. . . . It's fun to celebrate with those who live nearby. Events like these give you an opportunity to get to know folks you've only seen in passing. There's something special about breaking bread (eating) together. It bonds you. (Food does seem to have that effect, doesn't it?) Knowing and loving your neighbors is helpful in good times and in bad. There will come a day when those neighbors will need you—when a loved one passes, when a storm blows through and tears off someone's roof, when a child is sick. If you take time to get to know folks during the good times, it's easier to be there for them during the not-so-good times. Today, pause to thank God for neighborly affection.

Lord, it feels good to have people around me to share in my
life—in good, upbeat times and in times of deep distress.
Give me an affection for those surrounding me, I pray.
May I love my neighbors and participate
in their lives. Amen.

213

Thermostats

Let your steadfast love comfort me according to your promise to your servant.
PSALM 119:76 ESV

They save your neck on hot days and adjust the temperature for you on days when winter's chill nearly does you in. Automated thermostats are an amazing invention. You can set them for various times of day. They automatically adjust with changes in weather. You can even set them on vacation mode so your electric bill doesn't soar when you're out of town. Thermostats are a blessing, a true gift. (Can you even imagine what life was like for your grandparents and great-grandparents? If they were lucky, they had window units to cool the house during the hot days of summer.) You have it made, but sometimes you forget how blessed you are. Today, as you settle into that easy chair, cool air blowing from the vent above, pause to thank God for modern conveniences like thermostats!

Lord, it might sound silly, but I'm grateful for my AC and the thermostat that runs it. I have the ability to regulate temperatures in the house as I see fit, and I like that. Thanks for modern conveniences, Father. Amen.

214

Spare Tires

*Each day that we live, he provides for our needs
and gives us the strength of a young eagle.*
PSALM 103:5 CEV

~~~

You never need them. . .until you need them. Spare tires. They take up space in the rear of the vehicle, tucked away out of sight. But when the need arises, you thank God the tire is there. It's a gift that's been hidden until just the right moment. Isn't that what life is like? Some people treat others like spare tires. They don't call, they don't write, they don't text. . .until they need them. It's not a very good feeling, being a spare tire. Today, as you take the time to think through your relationships, ask the Lord to show you if you've been using anyone in this way. Also, take a look at folks who might be using you. It might be time for some forgiveness followed by tough love.

* * *

Father, I'll admit there are people I rarely call unless I need something from them. Please forgive me for that. Help me to forgive those who've taken advantage of my kindness in similar fashion, Lord. The only spare tire I hope to see from now on is the one in the back of my car. (And honestly, Lord, I don't really care to see that one either!) Amen.

215

Cool Breezes

In the beginning God created the
heavens and the earth.
GENESIS 1:1 NIV

You're hot. You're sweaty. You're ready to go inside, get out of the heat. Then just when you least expect it, a cool breeze rushes by. You lift your hair from your neck and drink in the moment. The unexpected breeze changes everything—your body temperature, your mood, your perspective. That's just what it's like when the Spirit of God blows through too. You're hot. You're agitated. You're annoyed with people. Then in rushes the Holy Spirit, and everything changes. You cool down. You see things through God's eyes. You're calm, cool, and collected. Today, as you think about the physical weather, ask the Lord to show you what areas of your life need "cooling." Then invite the Holy Spirit to blow through, bringing peace that only He can bring.

Father, thank You for the reminder that one breeze can
change everything. I ask You to breathe on my situation,
Lord, to blow through as only You can. I want to see as
You see. I want to feel as You feel. I want to know as
You know. Breathe on me, Spirit of God. Amen.

The Vast Ocean

*In the beginning God created the heavens and the earth.
The earth was barren, with no form of life; it was under
a roaring ocean covered with darkness. But the
Spirit of God was moving over the water.*
GENESIS 1:1–2 CEV

The tide rolls in and out, pushing and pulling against the shore. You stare out at the waves and try to stretch your vision to see as far as you can. But you can only see what you can see. Beyond your limited vision stretch miles and miles of water, wave upon wave, the great, vast unknown. It mesmerizes you, challenges your thinking, makes you want to hop on a cruise ship and take off into the abyss. More than anything, the ocean causes you to think about the Creator of it all, what He had in mind as He spun the waters into existence. He knew the role they would play. He knew you would one day sit here, staring out into the expanse. He knew. . .and still knows what's coming next. What a vast, unfathomable Creator!

*Father, You're beyond all comprehension. You created,
You planned, You knew. . .all things. You know what's out there,
over the horizon. You know the whys and wherefores of my life.
You know and You care, Lord. Thank You, Father! Amen.*

Happy News

*A messenger you can trust is just as
refreshing as cool water in summer.*
PROVERBS 25:13 CEV

～

You've just received the news and you're elated. It's a boy! A friend is in remission. The candidate you voted for has been elected. You got the job you've been waiting for. Your daughter is going to attend the university you attended. You're going to have a baby! The mortgage has been refinanced, lowering your payment. Yes, today the news is all good, and it feels like a cool drink on a hot summer day. It's just what you needed to get over whatever hurdle you've been trying to jump. Good news is like that. It shifts your focus and gives you a reason to celebrate even when you've been in a deep, dark place. It's a reminder that life goes on, that God really does care, that dreams can come true. Today, ponder the last bit of happy news you received. How did it change your life? Do you still feel that change even now?

*Father, thank You for interrupting my life time and time
again to deliver happy news. May I never forget that
good things are coming, that You care. And may I
never forget to deliver the ultimate good news that
You sent Your Son to die for all. Amen.*

218

Thirst

*The Spirit and the bride say, "Come!" And let the one
who hears say, "Come!" Let the one who is thirsty
come; and let the one who wishes take
the free gift of the water of life.*
REVELATION 22:17 NIV

You're parched. Dry. You've spent too much time in the heat.
You don't even realize how thirsty you are until it's almost
unbearable. Then it happens. Someone hands you a glass of
water. Beautiful, crystal-clear water. You tip the bottle toward
your lips, and the cool, delicious liquid soothes your mouth.
Relief floods over you as you take gulp after endless gulp. The
water is life-giving. It soothes. It brings you back from the abyss.
Thirst has driven you to the water's edge. In like manner, spiritual thirst drives you back to the Father's arms. When you're
weary, dry, bedraggled, turn to the One who can quench that
thirst. He's right there—Living Water—ready to pour Himself
out so you will never thirst again.

*Father, You have poured Yourself out on my behalf.
You love me. You gave Yourself for me. How can
I ever thank You? I'll never thirst again, Lord,
because of this amazing Living Water. Amen.*

Good Samaritans

*But a Samaritan, as he traveled, came where the man
was; and when he saw him, he took pity on him.*
LUKE 10:33 NIV

They stop when no one else stops. They help when no one else
helps. They give when no one else gives. They don't look at the
social status of the one they're helping—they give of themselves
to any and all who need assistance. These Good Samaritans are
more than just legends; they are people we know and love. The
world would be a dismal place without them. They are a gift
not just to those they help but to those of us who are watching
from a distance. We want to be like them, to do as they do, to
touch as they touch, to heal as they heal. Today, as you think
through all the Good Samaritans in your life—both the ones who
reached out to you at your lowest and those you've witnessed
helping others—ask for a double blessing from the Lord for
these special people.

*Lord, I ask You to bless the Good Samaritans in my life. You
know who they are, Lord. You see all they do. You feel their
heartbeat as they touch lives. Bless them, I pray, and give
them all they need to minister to others. Amen.*

Customers

But someday, people will again spend their silver to buy fields everywhere—in the territory of Benjamin, the region around Jerusalem and the towns of Judah, and in the hill country, the foothills to the west, and the Southern Desert. Buyers and sellers and witnesses will sign and seal the bills of sale for the fields. It will happen, because I will give this land back to my people. I, the LORD, have spoken.
JEREMIAH 32:44 CEV

They buy products, peruse store shelves, keep stores in business. They purchase auto insurance, hire plumbers, and order birthday cakes. They pay to have their hair cut, their nails polished, and their feet massaged. They're customers, and they are the foundation of society. In the world of supply and demand, these folks are a critical part of the equation. Without demand, there would be no need for supplies. If you work in a business that caters to customers, you know how important these relationships can be. Today, whether you're in customer service or a regular customer at a place of business, pray for both the business and the one in need of services. This unique relationship keeps money flowing and societies humming.

Father, thank You for local businesses that cater to customers. I pray blessings on both the supplier and the one in need of services. Amen.

221

Stability

Therefore, my beloved brothers, be steadfast, immovable,
always abounding in the work of the Lord, knowing
that in the Lord your labor is not in vain.
1 CORINTHIANS 15:58 ESV

She doesn't shift to the right or left when the winds of life blow.
She's not flighty in attitude or beliefs. She's stable. Consistent.
Dependable. And you want to be like her. You watch as she goes
through a hard season. You wonder if her faith will wane. She
holds tight. You observe as she faces a loss. She grieves but
doesn't give up. You find this admirable. Stability is a gift, and
it's one you want to wear close to your heart. A stable person
is rooted, grounded, safe. So you dig into the Word of God and
plant your roots deep. You draw close to the Lord and allow your
heart to beat in sync with His. There, in that quiet place, you
learn that stability is truly possible as long as you hold fast to
the hand of the Lord.

Lord, thank You for the reminder that I can be stable in mind,
body, and spirit. I don't have to waver when the storms of
life blow. I want to remain rooted in You, Father,
immovable, steadfast. Thank You for showing
me that this is possible. Amen.

222

Ice Cream

Oh, taste and see that the LORD is good!
Blessed is the man who takes refuge in him!
PSALM 34:8 ESV

∽

It's cool. It's tasty. It slips down your throat on a hot summer day or melts on your fingers causing a sticky mess. It's ice cream, and you love it. You choose your favorite—Rocky Road, Vanilla Velvet, Pistachio, Strawberries and Cream, Cherries Jubilee—and dive in. In that moment, as the cold, refreshing sweetness hits your lips, you're a kid again, standing at your mother's side after needling her to buy you an ice-cream cone. It's just as delicious now as it was then (though slightly less messy). You're in heaven, and all because of the gift of ice cream.

. . . .

Lord, it's such a simple pleasure, but I never want to take it for granted. I love ice cream. I have my favorite flavors. You know what they are. Truth is, I could eat ice cream every day and not get bored! Thanks for this sweet treat, Father. Amen.

EMS Workers

Jesus heard them and answered, "Healthy people don't need a doctor, but sick people do."
MATTHEW 9:12 CEV

⁓

Firemen. Paramedics. Police officers. These are the emergency response workers who come to your rescue when something unexpected and tragic occurs. With little thought to their own safety, they scale walls, lift and lug, offer any and all assistance not because they know and love you—because they don't—but because it's their job, their calling. These amazing people are gifts to their respective communities, but they're often overlooked. Today, spend some time praying for your local EMS workers. Then, just for fun, bake cookies or cupcakes, and take them up to the firehouse or the police station. Chances are really good you'll make someone's day when you honor them with this special treat. Most of all, treat them with the respect they deserve. What a blessing these fine people are!

Lord, thank You for placing the call to service on the hearts of these amazing EMS workers. I'm so grateful for every one. Please guard and protect them as they risk their lives to help others, Father. Keep them safe, I pray. Amen.

224

Pursuing Dreams

He said, "Listen to my words: When there is a prophet among you, I, the LORD, reveal myself to them in visions, I speak to them in dreams."
NUMBERS 12:6 NIV

❧

You chase after them like a kid chasing a puppy across the yard. They are yours and yours alone. You dreamed them up. You're the one to fulfill them. Only you can figure out how to get from point A to point B. There is One though, who longs to help you. He's actually the One who planted that dream in your heart to begin with, and He's hoping you'll take hold of His hand now so He can lead you toward fruition. God is the ultimate dream-giver. And He's for you not against you. Aren't you glad He's in the "pursuing" business? He pursued you, and now He's showing you how to chase after something you desire as well. What fun, this dream-gift!

* * *

Lord, I don't just want to chase after my dreams like they're some sort of elusive fantasy; I long to fulfill them, to see them through to fruition. I'll stick close to You and allow You to guide me so I don't waste any time in the pursuit of what You have for me. Here's my hand, Father. Take it and lead the way! Amen.

225

Spices

*As they sat down to eat their meal, they looked up and saw
a caravan of Ishmaelites coming from Gilead. Their camels
were loaded with spices, balm and myrrh, and they
were on their way to take them down to Egypt.*
GENESIS 37:25 NIV

Cinnamon. Garlic. Chili powder. Ginger. Lemon pepper. Dill. Red pepper flakes. These are the things you reach for when you want to add a little more zing to your dishes. Sure, salt and pepper have their place, but sometimes you just need more. Spices, many of which have their origins in ancient cultures, are a real gift. They liven up our food and keep things interesting. They are representative of various cultures, and many have a rich history. So which one is your favorite? Which ones do you avoid? Does your family have a particular favorite? The next time you reach for your spice rack, stop to think about where that spice came from. Do a little research. You might just find you're dipping into an ancient culinary well!

*Father, thank You for providing so many different
seasonings to spice up our foods. How dull life would be
if all foods looked and tasted alike. It's fun to have variety.
You're such a creative God, and I'm so grateful. Amen.*

226

Twilight Sleep

In peace I will lie down and sleep, for you alone,
LORD, make me dwell in safety.
PSALM 4:8 NIV

It's that dreamy, half-awake sleep that lulls you, coaxes you, woos you. Twilight sleep is a peaceful, calm place where God meets you half in, half out of consciousness. During these special minutes, you're completely at rest, completely at peace, but still open to the Holy Spirit's work. He whispers words of love over you and reminds you that you are special, unique, His. This is also the time for last-minute conversations with the Lord, spoken internally, not with your lips but with your heart. He hears you even now. As your eyes grow heavy, as you lay the day to rest, you have the full assurance that though you slumber, you are never alone. Even here, in this blissful state, God cradles you in His arms.

Father, I love those moments just before I doze off. I often meet You in those moments. I see You more clearly. Love You more deeply. Thank You for twilight sleep, Lord—that half-in, half-out state where I'm fully at peace and fully Yours. Amen.

227

Security

Do not be anxious about anything, but in everything,
by prayer and petition, with thanksgiving,
present your requests to God.
PHILIPPIANS 4:6 NIV

$\sim\!\!\!\sim$

Safe. Covered. Assured. Secure. This is how you feel whenever you've given your problems to the Lord. They're not yours to carry anymore. The weight has been lifted. Your hands are free to raise in praise. You can lift your shoulders once more. You're secure. Held tightly. Surrounded by His love. Not everyone understands this sort of security. Others are left hanging, fragile, vulnerable. You want to share the news with all of them—God can change this from the inside out. He can fix the unfixable, mend the unmendable. One by one, you approach your hurting friends and loved ones, ready to offer hope, to share your story, to stand as a witness to God's favor and strength. One day. One day your story will be seen in all its fullness. Until then, keep sharing your story so that others might find security in Him.

Father, may my testimony be a witness to all You're capable
of doing. I want others to experience Your goodness,
Your healing, Your safety. Help me as I share, I pray. Amen.

228

Tears

Those who sow with tears will reap with songs of joy.
PSALM 126:5 NIV

~~~

"Big girls don't cry." "Don't be a baby." "Pull yourself together." How many times have you heard those words? The world cries out, "Get it together!" while God says, "Come to Me. Let Me touch your heart. Let those tears flow. Be cleansed. Be made whole." So which will it be? Will you pull it together and pretend everything's okay when it's not? Will you pretend you're okay when you're not? Or will you run to Jesus and let those tears flow as He whispers words of comfort and freedom into your ear? He longs to heal you, you know, and tears play a role in that. So let them flow! Watch as God begins good work in you through the process.

* *

*Just call me a crybaby, Lord. If releasing emotions through
tears is what it takes to be rid of the pain of yesterday,
then I'll cry a river. I want to be healed. I want to be
whole. Let the tears flow, Father, and let Your
healing work be complete. Amen.*

Good Medicine

A cheerful heart is good medicine,
but a crushed spirit dries up the bones.
PROVERBS 17:22 NIV

Aren't you glad you live in the modern age, where medical advances are happening all around you? Researchers aren't just coming up with more pills, more injections—they're also finding that the best medicine in many cases is good, healthy eating combined with the right amount of exercise. These best medicines, they're learning, are what God provided all along. Today, as you ponder your health, take a look at what you're consuming. Does it provide health and wellness to your body? It might be time to take serious inventory to improve your health. Proper rest. Good food. The right amount of sunlight. Good supplements. These things will help you live a longer, healthier life. Just a little food for thought.

Father, thanks for the reminder that good medicine was there
all along in the form of healthy foods, fresh air, sunshine,
and rest. I needed that reminder, Lord! Amen.

230

Internet

So the word of God spread. The number of disciples in
Jerusalem increased rapidly, and a large number
of priests became obedient to the faith.
ACTS 6:7 NIV

⬿

What a remarkable gift the internet is. It connects people from
one side of the planet to the other and in nanoseconds! With the
push of a button, you can share a photo with a friend in Africa
or Asia. You can visit websites for individuals in Europe. You
can take a virtual tour of a home in Australia. The internet has
made the whole world accessible. It has also given researchers
and historians data at their fingertips. It has opened up the
world of ancestry/genealogy, connecting distant cousins who
didn't even know they were related. There's no way to know
all the effects, good and bad, the internet has had, but for the
most part we couldn't do without it! Today, thank the Lord for
the marvel of staying in touch in real time.

God, I'm grateful for instant access to information from
around the globe. I enjoy browsing the pages and gleaning
all I can. Thank You for keeping me connected, Lord.
And please, Father, protect all who venture out onto
the internet. Keep them safe, I pray. Amen.

231

Choice

*"But if serving the LORD seems undesirable to you, then choose
for yourselves this day whom you will serve, whether the gods
your ancestors served beyond the Euphrates, or the gods
of the Amorites, in whose land you are living. But as for
me and my household, we will serve the LORD."*
JOSHUA 24:15 NIV

You get to choose—what to eat for breakfast, what clothes to
wear, which car to drive, what job to accept. You can choose
to go to college or not, stick to a certain diet or not, or marry
a certain man. . .or not. These are all choices you can make.
Pause to think that through. Every day, you've made hundreds
of choices, many of which have passed by unnoticed. Choice,
itself, is a gift. Think of all the people in this world who have
no choices. They're forced to live a certain way, marry a certain
person, abide by the rules of others. They have no freedom to
choose. Today, take some time to pray for those who are trapped
in choiceless lives. May they find freedom! Then take the time
to thank God for the gift of choice.

*Father, thank You for giving me the freedom to choose.
I don't always make the right choices, Lord, but I promise
to keep trying to do my best. May I never take this
precious gift for granted, Father. Amen.*

232

Trust

Trust in the LORD with all your heart and lean not on your own understanding; in all your ways submit to him, and he will make your paths straight.
PROVERBS 3:5-6 NIV

It's hard to know whom to trust. You put your faith in someone, and then they pull the rug out from under you. You dare to trust again, only to be hurt once more. Then God comes along and asks you to trust Him. You're not sure. Is He trustworthy, or will He let you down like the others? You decide to give it a go. You release the things you've been clutching so tightly in your hands, trusting them to His care. . .and you're not disappointed. For the first time in a long time, you've found Someone who isn't lying when He says, "You can trust Me, kiddo." If He said it, you can take it to the bank. What a gift, this trustworthy God!

Father, I can trust You! How I love saying those words. I can trust You with the big things and the small things. I can trust You when I'm on the mountaintop or when I'm crawling on my belly through the valley. You won't let me down, Lord, and I'm so grateful. Amen.

233

Fast Food

Then he prayed again, and heaven gave rain,
and the earth bore its fruit.
JAMES 5:18 ESV

You're in a rush. No time to cook. No time to clean. You have places to be, people to see. But you're hungry. The kids are starving. What's a gal to do? You whip through the drive-through of a favorite fast-food restaurant, grateful for an easy option. No, it's not something you do very often, but on a day like today, you're grateful for the choice to find something easy and inexpensive. Whether you love it or hate it, the fast-food industry has made eating out easier. You can drive through and pick up a meal in less than five minutes then head on your way.

Lord, I don't want to be guilty of overspending on fast food,
but I am grateful for the option of occasionally
driving through to grab food in a hurry.

234

Family Collectibles

Love one another with brotherly affection.
Outdo one another in showing honor.
ROMANS 12:10 ESV

⟿

That quilt from your great-grandmother. Those dishes from your great-aunt. Those salt and pepper shakers from your mother. These and so many other collectibles fill your home and your heart. You look at them, and you're transported at once. You see yourself as a child at your great-aunt's home. She's using those very dishes. You imagine what it must have been like when your grandmother was a child, cozy under that quilt. These items are a gift, passed down from generations before. Today, take the time to thank God for them. Then take a look around your home. What items will you pass down to your children and grandchildren? Do they know the stories behind those items? This might be the perfect time to write down those stories.

God, I love the little knickknacks I've collected over the years, especially those with familial significance. What treasures they are! Help me to keep memories alive by preparing gifts for my loved ones too, Father. I want to keep the memories going from one generation to the next. Show me how to do that, I pray. Amen.

235

Military

*The L ORD is gracious and righteous; our God is full
of compassion. The L ORD protects the unwary;
when I was brought low, he saved me.*
PSALM 116:5–6 NIV

~~

They give up the comforts of home. They risk their lives, everyday comforts, and so much more to protect you all around the
globe. Our fine men and women of the military are, perhaps,
one of the greatest gifts we'll ever have. While you're sleeping
soundly, they're on guard, ready to step into battle should the
need call for it. They're missing their wives, husbands, parents,
children, and other loved ones, but they feel a strong calling
to do what they're doing for the good of the country they love.
And they do love their country. Otherwise, they'd never be in
this position in the first place. Today, as you pause to pray, lift
up a prayer of safety for those in the military. Pray for peace,
for their families, and for a hedge of protection around them.

* * *

*Father, I'm so grateful for those who've made the sacrifice to
serve in the armed forces. No matter what branch of service
they're in, I pray for safety, blessing, and comfort. Fill any
holes of loneliness with Your peace, Your presence,
Your love. Guard them, I pray. Amen.*

Workplace Friendships

Do you see a man skillful in his work? He will stand before kings; he will not stand before obscure men.
PROVERBS 22:29 ESV

Workplaces are as varied as the products and skills they represent. Some are cold and harsh. Others are abuzz with activity. Some are merely rooms where exhausted people shuffle to and fro, working until they drop. Others are a laugh a minute, with coworkers who are more like friends. No matter where you work, you're surrounded by people who've become like family to you. In many cases, workplace friendships are key to your survival because you're with these folks for more hours per day than many of your close friends or family members. So who have you developed a friendship with? Who can you trust? Who has your back? Who are you drawn to? Have you found a kindred spirit, someone who loves the Lord as you do? Are you witnessing to others with the Spirit of the Lord leading the way? Allow these amazing people, these gifts from God, to propel you forward in your faith as you face each new day together.

Lord, thank You for surrounding me with coworkers, even those I don't always agree with. Show me how to be the best possible friend in this situation, Lord. I want to be a witness for You while enjoying relationships with those You've placed in my path. Praise You, Lord. Amen.

Cheerfulness

A glad heart makes a cheerful face,
but by sorrow of heart the spirit is crushed.
PROVERBS 15:13 ESV

You pass by him in the hallway at work and he offers you more than a nod; a wonderful smile greets you. Later, you hear him chatting with his friends at lunch. Everyone seems to gather around him. He has everyone grinning now. Even when an in-office conflict arises later that afternoon, he's on it, calming people and bringing peace to the situation. He's a cheerful fellow, and people are drawn to him. It's not a fake, put-on cheerfulness. This comes from deep down inside, a true gift. And he knows just how to use it, as he moves from person to person, situation to situation. You enjoy watching him at work and play, and learn from his actions. Maybe, if you pay close attention, you can glean a bit of that cheer and spread it to others.

Lord, I want to be known as someone who cheers others.
May I bring a smile instead of worry lines to my coworkers'
faces. May I move with such cheerful ease that others want
to tap into what I have. Help me with this, I pray. Amen.

238

Bottled Tears

You have kept count of my tossings; put my tears
in your bottle. Are they not in your book?
PSALM 56:8 ESV

❧

Isn't it a remarkable notion that God has kept all of your tears in a bottle? How big is this bottle, anyway? Chances are pretty good you've cried a lot of tears in your life, especially if you count the first few years. Why do you suppose the Lord cares enough to count every tear and save it for all eternity? He's deeply concerned about your well-being. When your heart is broken, He longs to see it healed. But that doesn't mean tears are a bad thing. They're a gift, really. They provide a sense of release when your emotions are bottled up. They flow freely, offering a visible sign that you genuinely care about what's happening to you. And how precious, that the God of the universe cares about every tiny drop. Even now, across this great big planet, He's scooping tears into countless bottles. His love is that deep.

. . . .

Lord, thank You for caring so much. I couldn't begin to
count the number of tears I've cried in my life, but You know.
Perhaps one day I'll see the bottle You've been holding just
for me. Just thinking about it brings more tears
to my eyes. Praise You, Father. Amen.

People Who Walk with You in the Valley

*A friend loves at all times, and a brother
is born for adversity.*
PROVERBS 17:17 ESV

She's been there with you from the moment you got the news.
She grabbed tight to your hand and, with a squeeze, promised
to stick with you. And she has. As you went from depth to depth,
pain to pain, she traveled alongside you. She's more than just
a friend, she's your shadow in the valley, she's your voice when
you have none, your strength when yours has waned. She's
committed. She's not going to let go of your hand. And you're
so grateful. This sort of friend—the one who walks with you in
the valley—is a rare find, so thank God for her today. And ask
Him to show you how to be that kind of friend for others.

*Lord, I'm so grateful for the friends who go the distance
with me. They don't give up even when I'm in crisis mode.
They're standing firm, hand clutching mine, praying,
loving, giving. Thank You for these amazing
people, Father. Amen.*

240

Challenges

We are afflicted in every way, but not crushed; perplexed,
but not driven to despair; persecuted, but not
forsaken; struck down, but not destroyed.

2 Corinthians 4:8–9 esv

Most people wouldn't consider challenges a gift. Many would say they are hurdles, unnecessary burdens. But challenges provide ample opportunity to grow, and growth is a good thing. What challenges are you facing today? Do they seem overwhelming to you? Have they caused you to feel like giving up? Don't give up, and don't give in to fear, pain, or heartache. Take that challenge, the very thing that's causing so much turmoil, and give it to your heavenly Father. He's big enough to handle it. He will turn your situation around, though not likely in the way you envision it happening. God cares so much about you in good times and bad. He longs to use your hard times for His glory.

Lord, I confess I don't like challenges. I'd rather skip right
past them and live only for the good times. But I know that
my struggles are growing me into a mighty woman who trusts
You. So help me, I pray. I want to be an overcomer, even before
the battle is won. Help me to see myself as one, even
though the battle is still raging, Father. Amen.

241

Creativity

*Now the earth was formless and empty, darkness was over
the surface of the deep, and the Spirit of God
was hovering over the waters.*
GENESIS 1:2 NIV

Can you picture it? The earth has no shape, no form. Darkness covers everything, top to bottom, side to side. Over the water hovers the Spirit of God—God, the Creator, the Author, the Originator of all that is to come. With a word, He spoke the world into existence and then filled it with every living thing. His creative power created everything from nothing. And He's placed that same creativity in you. No, you won't be speaking literal worlds into existence, but you'll dream dreams, follow paths to places you've never been. You'll grow, learn, and develop skills, all with creative flair. Why? Because you're created in the image of your very creative Daddy-God. That creativity is inside of you because you're His. Where will you let this special gift take you today?

*Father, thank You for creating me to be creative. I want
to speak life into things just as You did when Your Spirit
hovered over the waters. May that creative spark live in
me. . .always. I praise You for what's to come, Lord. Amen.*

242

Appreciation for Something You've Done

We give thanks to God always for all of you,
constantly mentioning you in our prayers.
1 THESSALONIANS 1:2 ESV

You've sacrificed. You've given of your time, talents, and treasures. Your hard work has paid off. But you wonder if anyone will offer a pat on the back or even acknowledge you for all your hard work. Then he does. That one coworker who always seems to notice. That one friend at church who always sees when you've worked hard putting together a women's ministry event. She gives you a pat on the back. Someone else sends an "atta-girl" email; yet another sends a text. You don't sacrifice to receive praise, but there's something to be said for the encouragement a pat on the back can give. It feels good to be appreciated.

Father, there have been times I've worked so hard, and no
one seemed to notice. Thank You for the encouragement
I've received from those who are paying attention,
Lord. What a blessing they are to me. Amen.

243

Leadership

But Jesus called them to him and said, "You know that the rulers of the Gentiles lord it over them, and their great ones exercise authority over them. It shall not be so among you. But whoever would be great among you must be your servant, and whoever would be first among you must be your slave, even as the Son of Man came not to be served but to serve, and to give his life as a ransom for many."
MATTHEW 20:25-28 ESV

Sometimes you just have to pray that the people who've been put in leadership over you—bosses, pastors, politicians, and so on—are the right people for the job. You can't always be sure until you've walked the road with them for a while. A good leader is a terrific asset, a real gift to his or her workplace, church, community, and so on. Today, think about all of those in leadership over you. Pray for them. Then ask the Lord to develop leadership skills in you as well.

Father, thank You for good leaders.
They make the experience of following so much nicer.
Please bless those who lead, I pray. Amen.

244

Educators & Teachers

*"The student is not above the teacher,
nor a servant above his master."*
MATTHEW 10:24 NIV

God bless those who've been called to teach. Whether they work in public schools, private schools, universities, junior colleges, or as tutors or homeschool moms, educators are to be honored. They pour effort, knowledge, and direction into lives on a daily basis, often for little pay. These amazing people are a gift to all who learn from them. Today, pause to think of a teacher who's meant a lot to you, your child, or someone you know. Lift up a prayer for that teacher's well-being. Then, just for the fun of it, send her a little card or gift. Maybe a cookie or fruit bouquet. She'll be tickled pink. Honor her in front of her students so that all can see and celebrate her together. What fun you'll have, celebrating this special gift.

* * *

*God, today I lift up teachers before Your throne. Protect them,
encourage them, bring peace to any places of turmoil.
Most of all, bless them for the hard work they're doing, Lord.
What a blessing they are to all who enter their classroom!
I praise You for these wonderful gifts, Lord. Amen.*

245

School Cafeteria Workers

Whatever you do, work heartily,
as for the Lord and not for men.
COLOSSIANS 3:23 ESV

What a blessing these amazing men and women are. They tend to our children's bellies each and every day in the school lunchroom. They prep, they cook, they serve, they clean up, and all so that the children can have a healthy meal. School cafeteria workers often fly under the radar. They rarely receive notice or praise. Today, why not write a note or have your child write a note of thanks to the cafeteria workers at your local school? You'll make someone's day by offering up a few words of kindness and thanks. And while you're at it, think of others who work at the school—the janitor, for instance, or the nurse. They could probably use a note of thanks as well! What a gift these amazing people are to children across the globe.

Father, these awesome people work so hard.
Bless them, I pray. Sustain. Meet every financial
need. Thank You for surrounding our children
with people like these who love and care. Amen.

246

Change of Seasons

He made the moon to mark the seasons,
and the sun knows when to go down.
PSALM 104:19 NIV

We look at the changing of the seasons with awe and respect. God sure knows what He's doing as the summer morphs to autumn and autumn shifts to winter. When it comes to changing seasons in our personal lives, however, we're not always as trusting. We wonder what God's up to. We don't handle change well. The truth is this: the same God who shifts the seasons knows how to bring about change in your life. He's not moving things around to confuse or upset you. He's leading you toward newer, better, greater days ahead. So relax. Let the Creator do His creative work in you. You'll make it past this change and marvel at all He's done in your life.

. . . .

Father, I do trust You. It's not always easy when the winds are
shifting around me. I'm not keen on personal change, Lord.
But today I commit to trust Your work in my life even when I
don't understand. I know You have great things planned for
me, Father. I can't wait to see what lies ahead. Amen.

Preparedness

The other Israelite tribes organized their army and found
they had four hundred thousand experienced soldiers.
JUDGES 20:17 CEV

There's nothing like being prepared. You head into that meeting with all of your ducks in a row. You've charged the battery on your laptop so your presentation won't be interrupted. You've already thought through any questions they might ask, and you have answers. You've shut off your phone so that calls won't come through. You touched up your lipstick and gave your hair one last glance in the mirror before walking into the room. You're ready. You've done your due diligence. You're prepared. Of course, not everyone operates this way. Some folks show up at the last minute, so many things left undone. They do their best, but the presentation is lacking. Not you though. You have this down to a science. Being prepared is a gift, and it's one you plan to share with others.

Father, thank You for the gift of preparedness. I want to be
known as one who has her ducks in a row. With Your help,
Lord, I can tackle any task and stand before
others, ready to roll. Amen.

248

Work

*Serve wholeheartedly, as if you were serving the Lord,
not people, because you know that the Lord will
reward each one for whatever good they do,
whether they are slave or free.*
EPHESIANS 6:7–8 NIV

Have you ever considered the notion that work is a gift? Maybe it doesn't feel like it right now. Maybe you're overtaxed, exhausted, and hoping for a day off. But the process of getting up each morning and facing a particular task is a good one. God came up with the idea of work not to wear us out or make us earn our keep but to show us what we're capable of. There's a great reward for those who work hard. So where is your work leading you at this point in your life? What tasks lie ahead? Begin to see them as a joyful thing, an opportunity, a chance to show yourself that you have the goods. God has put great things inside you. Now step out and fulfill that destiny by working hard!

*Father, I don't always work as hard as I should.
Sometimes I slack off. Today I recommit myself to putting
my energy behind my tasks. I want to please You and
those I work for. You are showing me that I have
the goods, Lord, so I'm stepping out! Amen.*

249

Learning

"Hear my words, you wise men;
listen to me, you men of learning."
JOB 34:2 NIV

The ability to learn is a gift, one you never lose no matter how many years pass by. You are a forever-student, always on a learning curve, and that's a good thing. God has so many things to teach you—different lessons for different seasons. Are you a ready student, or do you rebel at the notion that you're still in the classroom of life? Today is a good day to take inventory. What areas of your life (what courses, as it were) still need improvement? How can you be a better woman, wife, mother, daughter, friend, coworker? Ask God to put you in His classroom and teach you whatever lessons need to be learned so you can better represent Him to a watching world.

God, I don't relish the idea of going back to school. I wasn't
always the best student. But I'll strive to learn all You have to
teach me, Father, because I want to shine my light for others.
So put me in the classroom. Step up to the chalkboard.
I'm ready, Lord. I'm Your student for life. Amen.

250

Productivity

Whatever you do, work heartily,
as for the Lord and not for men.
COLOSSIANS 3:23 ESV

She's one of the most productive people you've ever met. You've never known anyone who could accomplish all she does. You're a little envious because she always manages to get the attention of others, and usually in a good way. You wonder how she does it. Is she superhuman? Truthfully, some people are just wired to be productive. They move at lightning speed and accomplish things that others could only dream of. Maybe you're not wired that way. Maybe you're more like the turtle, getting your tasks done but in a slow and steady fashion. Don't get frustrated. You're productive too. And it's not a race, after all. There are no winners and losers, only participants.

Lord, I want to be productive like some others whom
I know. Help me to increase my productivity, I pray.
May I accomplish more for Your Kingdom, Father. Amen.

251

Technology

"For nothing will be impossible with God."
LUKE 1:37 ESV

Computers. Laptops. Tablets. Smart TVs. Smart phones. Smart cars. Apps. Digital streaming. Virtual assistants. Voice recognition software. Online shopping. iCloud. The things available to us today are remarkable! None of these things existed even one generation back. (Look how far we've come!) Aren't you grateful to live in the age of modern technology? With the touch of a button you can do what you like, have what you like, order what you like. Of course, as with most good things, there are always risks, particularly when it comes to your safety and financial security, but you're savvy. You're careful. You see technology for what it is, an amazing gift to help you grow and develop as a person and usable to spread the Gospel too.

Lord, what an amazing tool I have at my disposal.
Technology is advancing even now. I can barely keep up.
Thank You for giving us a way to reach others with the
Gospel message. With the click of a button, I can tell others
about what You've done in my life. Remarkable! Amen.

252

Payday

"But as for you, be strong and do not give up,
for your work will be rewarded."
2 CHRONICLES 15:7 NIV

You waited for days as your bank account dwindled. Finally, the moment arrived. Payday! The money was deposited into your account, and you could breathe a sigh of relief. The rent could be paid. So could the electric bill. The car payment would have to wait until your next payday, but things were looking hopeful. It's fun to look forward to the day when money is deposited, but you're cognizant of the fact that God is your source. He's given you an amazing job (thank You, Lord!), but ultimately He's the One who makes provision to cover those bills. So take a moment to thank Him for His provision. He has you covered and not just on payday!

Lord, I'm always so excited when there's money in the bank.
I can breathe a sigh of relief. Thank You for the reminder that
I don't have to wait until payday to trust You, Lord. You're
taking care of me 365 days a year. Bless You for that. Amen.

253

Wit

A wise man is full of strength,
and a man of knowledge enhances his might.
PROVERBS 24:5 ESV

He's witty. Funny. Clever. He knows how to crack a joke and deliver a punchline. You're tickled every time he opens his mouth, because you anticipate what he's going to say. People with wit are a real gift to others. They can help you forget your troubles and remind you that sometimes it really is just mind over matter. So what about you? Would people consider you witty? Maybe it's time to sharpen that wit so that you can become a ray of sunshine to people who are hurting. Use that wit to bless, never hurt. Ask God to lead you to those in need of cheering.

Father, I love witty people. They're so fun (and funny).
Thanks for blessing me with so many. Today I ask that
You sharpen my wit. I want to lift spirits, to bring
encouragement, to retain humorous tidbits I can
share. Will You help me with that,
Lord? Thanks! Amen.

254

Quiet Retreats

Seek the LORD and his strength;
seek his presence continually!
1 CHRONICLES 16:11 ESV

～

There's something about the word *retreat* that makes you feel so peaceful inside. When you retreat, you're backing up, away from the war, away from the chaos. You're making an announcement: "I've checked out for a while. See you when I get back." You're in a safe, quiet place where no one can disturb you, where cell phones don't exist, where text messages and emails can wait for another day. Best of all, you're in a place of quiet so God can speak to your heart. He has a lot to say, you know. He's been waiting for things to quiet down so He could whisper a few things into your heart.

* * *

Lord, I love stepping away from my chaotic life. Retreating, backing up, stepping away from the chaos. . .this is critical to my survival. Thanks for the reminder that quiet retreats aren't selfish; they're a gift from You. You long for me to draw close to You, Lord. I choose to do that even now. Amen.

Inventions

*For by him all things were created, in heaven and on earth,
visible and invisible, whether thrones or dominions or rulers
or authorities—all things were created through him
and for him. And he is before all things,
and in him all things hold together.*
COLOSSIANS 1:16–17 ESV

You marvel at each new invention. Some are technology-driven;
others are marvelous creations you'd never thought of before.
You wonder how some people think like that, how they come up
with the ideas that they do. They've been gifted from on high to
create, to spin their magic, to marvel the masses. And you get to
benefit from their creations. Each one makes life a little easier,
your days a little smoother, your journeys a little less stressful.
With each new app, every GPS device, every modern marvel,
you are the beneficiary. So sit back. Let the creators create. Let
the imaginative thinkers dream up their next great inventions.
You'll be the one enjoying the gift once it's ready to be given.

*Father, thank You for each new invention. Continue to pour
out creative juices on all the inventors out there—those
working in technology and every field beyond. Give them
exciting new ideas that will benefit humankind.
Stir them to action, Lord. Amen.*

256

Ability to Retain

Let the wise listen and add to their learning,
and let the discerning get guidance.
PROVERBS 1:5 NIV

Maybe you're at an age where you feel like you can't retain anything. Stories, lessons, life skills go in one ear and out the other. Did you know that God created you to learn and to retain information? You can grow and develop that skill. Wherever you feel a lack, ask God to fill in the gap. He will do it. He longs for you to acquire wisdom, and that only comes from submitting yourself to the process. So pretend you're a sponge! Soak it up. Then, when you think you can't take anymore, start over and soak up more of His Word. Write scriptures down. Put them up on your mirror, your desk, your wall. You'll be surprised at how much you retain simply through repetition. What are you waiting for? You have a lot of learning to do!

Lord, I want to be a sponge soaking up more and more of Your
Word. Help me, I pray. Give me the skills to learn and retain
more with each passing day. Thank You, Father. Amen.

257

Risks

Do not fear what you are about to suffer. Behold, the devil is about to throw some of you into prison, that you may be tested, and for ten days you will have tribulation. Be faithful unto death, and I will give you the crown of life.
REVELATION 2:10 ESV

No risk, no reward. You've heard that expression before. Of course, you would prefer the rewards without the risks, thank you very much. Risking—money, time, effort—doesn't always pay off. But you're willing. God has called you to risk it all for His Kingdom, and you're a willing participant. So what does this look like in the real world? It might mean risking some friendships now that you're living for the Lord. Not everyone will understand why you're drawing close to Him. It might also mean trusting God with your finances, tithing, giving money to missionaries. Whatever He calls you to do, you can trust Him. He's a good, good Father, and the rewards for your risks will be great.

I'd never thought of risks as a gift before, Lord, but now I see that they are. When I risk, there's a payoff. It's frightening, I must admit, but I know I can trust You. Show me how to submit even if it feels risky, Father. I humble myself and give myself over to the process. Amen.

258

Inseparable

*Neither height nor depth, nor anything else in all
creation, will be able to separate us from the love
of God that is in Christ Jesus our Lord.*
ROMANS 8:39 NIV

One of the finest gifts you'll ever receive is the assurance that
nothing you ever do will separate you from the Lord God. He
commits to an inseparable love for you. This doesn't give you
the freedom to test the theory to its limits, but if you do mess
up—and everyone does—you can rest assured He will forgive
you. You haven't lost His love. You don't have to come crawling
back on your belly, terrified He'll treat you with shame. You're His
daughter, His child, and He adores you. Today, take inventory.
Is there an area of your life you've been unwilling to share with
Him because you're afraid you will lose His love? Open up and
share from the heart. God's not going anywhere.

*Father, I come to You with every sin revealed, every flaw laid
bare before You. I know You love me, and I'm not afraid
to confess what I've done. Please forgive me for the times
I've broken Your heart. I recommit myself to You,
Father. Thank You for loving me. Amen.*

Trustworthiness

The works of his hands are faithful and just;
all his precepts are trustworthy.
PSALM 111:7 ESV

⤳

You give her the key to your house and don't fret over it. She's trustworthy. You loan him your car for the afternoon and don't give it a second thought. He's not going to drive off to the great unknown. He's trustworthy. There are many in your life who have proven their trustworthiness to you. You've watched them operate for years and have no doubts. Their trustworthiness is a gift. Now it's time to take inventory. Do others feel they can trust you? Do you hold on to their secrets without blabbing? Do you return what they've loaned you? Have you committed yourself to the friendship at any cost? A trustworthy friend is a friend for life, after all.

* *

Lord, thank You for placing so many trustworthy people in my life. I'm so grateful, Father. I want to be counted as one who can be trusted. If there are areas of my life I need to work on, I submit myself to the process, Lord. Help me, I pray. Amen.

260

Upward Call

Brothers, I do not consider that I have made it my own.
But one thing I do: forgetting what lies behind and straining
forward to what lies ahead, I press on toward the goal for
the prize of the upward call of God in Christ Jesus.
PHILIPPIANS 3:13–14 ESV

God's call is upward. There's forward motion. He's taking you someplace, and it's beyond where you are right now. Maybe you look at how far you've already come and think, *Whew! I don't know if I can go much further.* Hang on to your hat, sister! If you think this life you're currently living is grand, you haven't seen anything yet. He's taking you further, higher, into greater depths with Him. And He's bringing others with you, so hold tight to the hands of those you love. God has amazing things planned for you. It won't be long before you see for yourself.

Lord, I'm giddy with anticipation as I think about your
upward call. I'm already so blessed, Father. I'm willing to
go where You lead. I'm bolstering my courage for
the journey ahead. Lead me, I pray. Amen.

Personalized Gifts

*Then the servant brought out gold and silver jewelry and
articles of clothing and gave them to Rebekah; he also
gave costly gifts to her brother and to her mother.*
GENESIS 24:53 NIV

❧

A gift arrives in the mail. You open it, and you're tickled to see
a coffee cup with your name on it. Or maybe it's a box of note-
cards specific to what you're going through. The friend who
sent this gift knows you well. She knew just what to order to
make your day. She knows your favorite scent of bath soap, your
love for baking, and your passion for animals. So she chooses
accordingly. Those dachshund salt and pepper shakers? She
really outdid herself with those! In short, she pays attention to
the little things that delight you. Her personalized gifts make
you feel special. And now you want to return the favor. How
can you bless her in return? What sorts of things does she like?
It's time to hit the World Wide Web to hunt for a special gift!

*Lord, thank You for personalized gifts. They mean so much
to me. I want to pay attention to others as my friends have
done for me. Show me how to personalize a gift to
bring a smile to a friend's face, I pray. Amen.*

262

In Abundance

Mercy, peace and love be yours in abundance.
JUDE 1:2 NIV

God loves to lavish gifts on His children. He doesn't give things out by the thimbleful. No, He pours out mercy, peace, and love. . . in great abundance. It's like a river, flowing from the very throne room of God. He's an over-the-top giver, hoping to "wow" you with each new offering. So what has He given you lately? What are you most thankful for? Why not spend some time letting Him know how grateful you are? And while you're at it, think of ways that you can be an over-the-top blesser. Choose a special person, charity, or ministry. . .then give abundantly.

Lord, I love Your heart for Your kids! You don't just bless us. . .
You double and triple bless us! You share with such lavish
abundance that it takes my breath away. I want to learn
from You, Father, so I can bless others with that same
kind of abundance. Fill me with ideas, I pray. Amen.

263

Observant

*See what kind of love the Father has given to us, that we
should be called children of God; and so we are. The reason
why the world does not know us is that it did not know him.
Beloved, we are God's children now, and what we will be has
not yet appeared; but we know that when he appears we
shall be like him, because we shall see him as he is.*
1 JOHN 3:1–2 ESV

The world is watching. They see how you respond when others
hurt you. They notice when you turn the other cheek. They're
watching closely when you stand firm on an issue you're passionate about. They're observing—and not just out of curiosity. People want to know why you're so different, why you
have the beliefs you do. They're dying to know how you can
treat coworkers with such love, even when people take you for
granted or talk about you behind your back. They see Jesus in
you, and they like what they see whether they're bold enough
to admit it or not.

*Father, I know people are watching my relationship
with You. May I bring honor to You in how I live
and how I love others. Help me, Lord. Amen.*

264

A Secret Place

Whoever dwells in the shelter of the Most High will rest in the shadow of the Almighty. I will say of the LORD, "He is my refuge and my fortress, my God, in whom I trust."
PSALM 91: 1–2 NIV

God whispers, "Come away with Me." He extends His hand and leads you to the secret place, the inner chamber, where you spend time in His Word and in worship. There, in that inner sanctum, you deal with issues of the heart, things that have been troubling you. You pour out your love, your passions, your concerns, your worries. He soothes, pacifies, restores, comforts. You rest awhile in His presence, dwelling in His shelter for as long as you can before stirring. In those moments, He's more than just a refuge or a fortress; He's your Abba-Father. He's your Daddy-God. And He adores His daughter with a love beyond compare.

I love our secret place, Lord. It's just You and me, Father. No one else. We share. We hope. We love. And when I rise from that place, I'm made new once again, ready to face a new day. Thanks for spending time with me, Lord. Amen.

265

Windows

*After forty days Noah opened a window
he had made in the ark.*
GENESIS 8:6 NIV

～

They provide a view to the outside world, a glimpse into the great beyond. On the other side of the glass, you see flowers blooming, butterflies flitting, cars zooming, and children playing. Windows are a gift. They fuel the imagination and keep you from feeling penned in. When you open them, fresh air blows through the house. (This was probably an important part of Noah's story.) When you close them, you feel safe. Whether you're riding in a car, an airplane, a cruise ship, or sitting at home on your living room sofa, there's a window nearby. How frightening life would be without a way to see outside! Aren't you grateful for a glimpse of the outside world even on days when you have to stay home?

* * *

*I need glimpses of what's going on beyond my own little life,
Lord. I love to see the neighbors mowing the grass or children
riding their bikes down the sidewalk. I love opening windows
on a breezy day to let fresh air in. What bliss, Lord. Amen.*

266

Stepping Away from a Quarrel

As for the one who is weak in faith, welcome him,
but not to quarrel over opinions.
ROMANS 14:1 ESV

You have a right to your opinion even if others disagree with you. You can express it in love. Opinions are a gift. A freedom. An opportunity to speak truth as it is revealed to you. But opinions, loudly voiced, can lead to quarrels, and quarrels can result in broken relationships. While it's okay to have a difference of opinion, God wants you to keep your cool so the friendship stays intact. The ability to step away from a quarrel is a gift, an important one. Not everyone can take a deep breath and back down when things are getting heated. What about you? Do you cool off quickly or lose it? Maybe this is a good day to ask God to give you the gift of cooling down.

Father, I don't want to set off on a course to prove myself right
or to sway others to my opinion if it means I'm going to end
up wrecking the friendship we've built. Forgive me for
the times I've let things get out of hand, Lord.
Cool me down, I pray. Amen.

Precision & Order

But all things should be done decently and in order.
1 CORINTHIANS 14:40 ESV

❦

She's so precise. Everything is measured, calculated. She checks and double-checks. Then just when you think she's done, she measures again. That's why her quilts are so perfect. That's why the tile floor she laid looks so good. That's why the picture she hung on the wall is level. She has a knack for perfection and keeps at it until all her ducks are in a perfect row. You? Not so much. Sometimes you slap things together and hope for the best then wonder why your project didn't quite turn out the way you had planned. Precision is an ability, one that can be acquired by trial and error, but it's also a gift. Today, ask God to make you more precise—in your work, in your cleaning, and in the projects you tackle. He'll be happy to work with you on this project!

Lord, I need more precision in my life. I'm a little slaphappy sometimes, just throwing things together. Bring order where I lack order. Bring precision where I lack precision. Hone me, I pray. Make me more like You, Father. Amen.

268

Energy

"But you will receive power when the Holy Spirit comes on you; and you will be my witnesses in Jerusalem, and in all Judea and Samaria, and to the ends of the earth."
ACTS 1:8 NIV

～

You don't feel like it. You're worn out. You've had a hard day. It's just one more thing to do in a never-ending list of things to do. You'd rather not, thank you very much. The truth is you just don't have the energy to face one more thing. But what is energy, anyway? Is it physical or mental? Can you muster it up on days when you're worn out? Perhaps it's both. When you're worn down emotionally, it's hard to keep on keeping on. But take a look at today's verse. We're promised power (energy) when the Holy Spirit comes on us. In the spirit realm, He can accomplish what we cannot. In fact, He can empower us to the point where we're ready to spread the Gospel. Now that's miraculous energy!

* *

Father, I get so weary at times. I just want to crawl into bed and pull the covers over my head. Thank You for the reminder that power, energy, wherewithal come from Your Spirit. Today I ask for a double dose, Lord! I want to impact the kingdom for You. Amen.

Truth-Tellers

Rather, speaking the truth in love, we are to grow up
in every way into him who is the head, into Christ.
EPHESIANS 4:15 ESV

If you've raised children, you know what it's like to hear little white lies. Some kids are skilled tale-tellers. It's such a novelty to find a child—or adult—who never lies. He's a truth-teller, sometimes spilling the brutal truth. What about you? Were you the sort to tell white lies or one with a stiff backbone, always telling the truth? If so, did you/do you speak the truth in love? It's possible to deliver hard messages in soft packages, after all. Truthfulness is a gift you give yourself and others. Its delivery is part of the package. If you're in the habit of telling white lies, it might be time to confess that to the Lord and ask for His deliverance. Though it might seem small to you, it really matters to Him.

Father, may I be truthful in all my ways, always bringing
honor to You with my words. Please remove the temptation
to lie, Lord. Cleanse me of that, and point me in
the direction of truth. Amen.

The New Has Come

*Therefore, if anyone is in Christ, the new creation
has come: The old has gone, the new is here!*
2 CORINTHIANS 5:17 NIV

Maybe someone from your past has thrown something in your
face. They're reminding you who you used to be, what you used
to do, how you used to live. They don't want to believe you're
a new creation. They're not buying it. But you know better.
You've strengthened your resolve. Nothing could ever tempt
you to turn back to your old ways. The new has come—a new
heart, new outlook, new perspective. A new hope, new vision,
new energy. You're a new creation with motivation to move
forward not backward. How will your old friend be convinced?
There's only one way. You have to live it out.

*Father, I'm not going back. You've made all things new in my
life. The past doesn't even compare! Why would I turn back to
my old ways? Thank You for making me a new creation. I have
so much to look forward to, Lord! Bless You for new life. Amen.*

271

Through

When you pass through the waters, I will be with you; and when you pass through the rivers, they will not sweep over you. When you walk through the fire, you will not be burned; the flames will not set you ablaze.

ISAIAH 43:2 NIV

The word *through* is one of the finest words in the Bible. God isn't just leading you *to* places, He's leading you *through* them. Obstacles you thought you couldn't overcome, addictions you felt sure you'd never beat, relationships that seemed impossible, God's bringing you through. When you go *through* something, you don't stick around long enough for the icky stuff to stick to you. *Through* is a word of movement. You keep going right through the bad and into the good. You don't linger. You beat it out of there and get to the other side. So what's God bringing you through right now? You can rest assured He's taking you all the way.

Thank You for taking me through, God! What a gift this tiny little word is. I don't have to get stuck in the miry clay. You're taking me through. Bless You, Father! Amen.

272

The Flavors of Fall

Your robes are all fragrant with myrrh and aloes and cassia.
From ivory palaces stringed instruments make you glad.
PSALM 45:8 ESV

Pumpkin. Ginger. Cinnamon. Nutmeg. Caramel. Brown sugar. These are the flavors of fall, and you love them whether they're in your coffee, pie, cake, or other tasty desserts. There's something about the combination of these scents that makes you a little giddy in a good way. You look forward to autumn in part because of the flavors you know you'll get to enjoy. So which one is your favorite? How do you enjoy using it? Which could you do without? Maybe it's time to head to the store to pick up a few spices in preparation for the weeks ahead. Holidays are coming, after all. There will be baking to do, new recipes to try out. So get after it! And while you're at it, pick up more coffee. Chilly days call for warm treats.

* *

Lord, I just love the flavors of fall! Pumpkin lattes,
gingerbread, brown sugar coffee cake, cinnamon rolls.
Yum. I'm so grateful for all these wonderful, delicious,
tasty treats. If only I could enjoy them year-round!
(Oh wait. . .I can!) Thanks, Lord. Amen.

273

The Power of Two

*Two are better than one, because they have
a good return for their labor.*
ECCLESIASTES 4:9 NIV

~

Two are better than one. Oh sure. You think you can do it all by yourself. And you've tried. Many times you've tried. But today, take the time to invite a second person—the Lord of Creation—into your plan. Together, the two of you will work miracles! With His help, you'll leap mountains, you'll forge wildernesses, you'll ford streams. With His hand in yours, you'll see farther, hear better, taste and see things yet to come. God wants to give you a fantastic gift, the power of His presence. He has huge plans for this duo, creative plans, massive plans beyond your comprehension, so don't delay. What a mighty duo you'll be!

*Lord, why would I ever want to walk away from You?
You're the "dynamic" in this dynamic duo. You're the only
reason I've ever accomplished anything, Father. I don't know
why You love me so much, Lord, why You've stuck with me
through thick and thin, but I'm so grateful. Without You,
I would be nothing. Together, we are invincible!
Okay, You were invincible even without me,
but You know what I mean. Amen.*

274

Autumn

"They do not say in their hearts, 'Let us fear the LORD our God, who gives the rain in its season, the autumn rain and the spring rain, and keeps for us the weeks appointed for the harvest.'"
JEREMIAH 5:24 ESV

It's the season when things begin to die. Flowers fall from the vine. Leaves float from the trees. And as you watch them, you feel an odd sense of foreboding as if something's ending in your life with no hint of resurrection. Oh, lift your eyes today! Autumn is a glorious season. Yes, some things are coming to an end, but look at the beauty left behind. So much color! So much aroma! The same is true in your life. Your "autumn" is filled with heaping piles of colorful leaves, a vivid reminder that the work you've done up to this point mattered. It helped. It changed people and situations. Don't worry about what's coming next. Relax in the comfort of your autumn, and bask in the assurance that the same God who worked through you in your summer season has amazing things around the bend.

Lord, I'm not afraid of autumn. Things are winding down, but that's okay. I know You have more out there for me, Father. Right now I'm just going to relax and enjoy where I'm at. Amen.

Sunset

*The Mighty One, God, the Lord, speaks and summons
the earth from the rising of the sun to where it sets.*
PSALM 50:1 NIV

The brilliant colors take your breath away as they morph right before your eyes. What started out as a pink and blue sky melds into crimson and orange. Then, just about the time you're sure the colors will settle, they morph again—this time to vibrant hues of gold and red. Before long, the sun is slipping over the horizon, shadows of the evening following. You watch it all, your heart in your throat, as the magnificence of what you've just witnessed settles over you. God, the almighty Creator of all, designed that sunset in all its brilliance. You were blessed to watch the change in colors. The same scene will repeat itself tomorrow, of course, and the day after that as well. The colors will be slightly different, their hues in varying shades of day-meets-night. But someone somewhere will be watching in breathtaking awe.

*Lord, I see Your hand at work in the sunset. Every evening,
as You put the sun to sleep, You put on a theatrical show,
a display of Your brilliance. Those colors delight me, Father.
They leave me breathless, in awe of what a magnificent
Creator You are. Thank You for the gift of sunsets, Lord. Amen.*

276

Nature

"But ask the beasts, and they will teach you; the birds of the heavens, and they will tell you; or the bushes of the earth, and they will teach you; and the fish of the sea will declare to you. Who among all these does not know that the hand of the LORD has done this? In his hand is the life of every living thing and the breath of all mankind."

JOB 12:7–10 ESV

꩜

All of nature proclaims the greatness of God, from the early morning dew to the fish in the streams. Every living thing was created by the Lord for our enjoyment and for His good pleasure. This is especially marvelous to witness during the changing of the seasons. There's a sense of anticipation as summer shifts to autumn. The leaves, the trees, the very ground beneath us declares the glory of God. And we bear witness to it all, joyous spectators as life transforms around us. The Lord is at work even now. What is He transforming in the world around you? Take a look, and marvel at what He's doing.

Father, I see Your hand at work in the birds above and the fish below. I see You moving in the broken branches of the tree and the flowing waters of the brook. You're always working, Lord, and doing a fine job! Amen.

277

Colors

"Moreover, you shall make the tabernacle with ten curtains of fine twined linen and blue and purple and scarlet yarns; you shall make them with cherubim skillfully worked into them."
EXODUS 26:1 ESV

Have you ever wondered what colors were like in the Garden of Eden? Were the trees vibrant green with blossoming flowers in pink, yellow, purple, and white? Did the animals appear in varying shades of brown, black, and gray? Were the waters crystal clear or shining teal? We won't know the full scope of God's imagination when it comes to the color scale until we get to heaven, but He's given us a glimpse when we look at the world around us. The changing of the leaves in fall—morphing from green to red, then golden-orange to brown. The colors of the foods we eat—lemon yellow, avocado green, raspberry red, tangerine orange. This world is alive with the gift of color.

Lord, I'm so grateful for colors! I have my favorites, of course, but I'm tickled pink (pun intended) that You took the time to create such a vibrant, colorful world. Thank You for stirring our imaginations with this amazing gift. Amen.

278

Determination

But the one who endures to the end will be saved.
MATTHEW 24:13 ESV

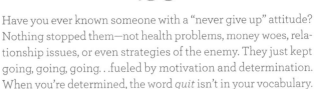

Have you ever known someone with a "never give up" attitude? Nothing stopped them—not health problems, money woes, relationship issues, or even strategies of the enemy. They just kept going, going, going...fueled by motivation and determination. When you're determined, the word *quit* isn't in your vocabulary. Your resolve is set. You have a firmness of purpose. And that purpose propels you time and time again. What is your purpose? What's propelling you? Do you have a can-do attitude? If so, then thank God for this gift, for it will see you far in life.

Lord, thank You for the reminder that my determination comes from a deep sense of resolve. It's not something I drum up on my own. When I'm aware of my purpose, I have goals. I have a particular sense of direction. I'm determined and won't stop no matter what obstacles appear in front of me. Steel my resolve today, I pray. Amen.

Cooperation

"Do two walk together, unless they have agreed to meet?"
AMOS 3:3 ESV

Don't you love cooperative people? They don't put up a fuss, don't demand their own way, and they're willing to work for the good of the team, not for their own good or glory. When things get rough, they keep going, ready to make things better. A person who cooperates is a gift. She's a blessing to those she works alongside. So what about you? Are you a team player, someone who cares more about the group outcome than her own personal good? Do people ask you to join their efforts then applaud you for not demanding your own way? A cooperative friend is a friend indeed. What a gift!

Lord, sometimes people have to rein me in. I like to take charge of things. I'm not always the most cooperative. Teach me to be a team player, Father. I want to learn to cooperate to the fullest. Together, we will perform amazing feats with Your help, Lord. Thank You for showing me how to better myself to benefit others. Amen.

280

Cuddling

His left arm is under my head
and his right arm embraces me.
SONG OF SOLOMON 8:3 NIV

It's a lazy autumn day and you feel like cuddling, so you reach for that little one and snuggle him close. Or maybe you coax your dog onto the sofa for some tickles and a scratch behind the ear. Maybe you talk your hubby into joining you on the sofa with the game playing in the background on the TV. There's something very comforting about having someone—or something—to cuddle. Cuddling is an act of love, of sweetness. It says, "I care enough about you to just sit right here and love on you." The dishes can wait. Texting can wait. You need the comfort that only cuddling can bring, and so does the one receiving your affection. Cuddling is a gift, one we all need from time to time.

. . . .

Lord, thank You for giving me opportunities to physically
express love to those in my world. I love snuggling,
cuddling, giving little hugs and kisses. What a
precious way to share love with those I care
about. I'm grateful for each one, Father. Amen.

Perseverance

*Blessed is the man who remains steadfast under trial,
for when he has stood the test he will receive the crown of
life, which God has promised to those who love him.*
JAMES 1:12 ESV

Never stop. Never ever stop. No matter what obstacles you face, don't give in, don't give up. Keep putting one foot in front of the other. That's your motto, and you follow it in good times and bad. Perseverance has become your friend. Your determination is admirable. But did you ever stop to consider the notion that perseverance is also a gift? Who put that desire to keep going inside your heart? Who rouses you each morning when you would rather be sleeping? Who nudges you when you're ready to quit? The Lord longs for you to overcome in every area, and the only way you're going to do that is if you keep on keeping on. So grab that gift and keep moving. Terrific things lie ahead if you will only keep going.

*Lord, I want to persevere, no matter what I face. It's not
always easy. I definitely need Your help. Give me the
determination and the courage to keep going, especially
when I feel like quitting. May I never ever give up. Amen.*

Wisdom & Knowledge

"Give me wisdom and knowledge, that I may lead this people, for who is able to govern this great people of yours?"
2 CHRONICLES 1:10 NIV

Are wisdom and knowledge the same thing? Perhaps you've never given that question any thought, but they are slightly different. Wisdom is something that comes from God—revelation from the Holy Spirit. Knowledge, on the other hand, can be acquired and increased by studying. There are many knowledgeable people in this world who have no godly wisdom at all. If you want to go far in this life, it's important to be both wise and knowledgeable. Draw close to God, and He will give you the wisdom of the ages. Do all you can to increase in knowledge—study to show yourself approved—and watch as God grows you into a mighty woman, capable of leading others.

Lord, I get it. I can develop my academic skills, I can further my education, but without wisdom from on high, I can only go so far. You have so much to teach me that I can't learn in school. I will acquire wisdom by sitting at Your feet. So that's what I choose to do today, Father. I'm drawing close so that I might grow in wisdom and so You can use me to reach others. Praise You. Amen.

283

Scars

Then he said to Thomas, "Put your finger here,
and see my hands; and put out your hand, and place it
in my side. Do not disbelieve, but believe."
JOHN 20:27 ESV

They don't look or feel like gifts to you. You don't wear them as a badge of honor. In fact, you do your best to cover them up with makeup or clothes. Scars are obvious signs of a prior injury or surgery and are often labeled as unsightly. You don't like to look, because looking reminds you of the pain that surgery caused. But today, consider a different notion: that scars are a gift. Sure, they're a reminder of a painful time, but more than that, they're proof that the body eventually heals. It sews itself back together, and the healed spot is stronger, tougher than ever. That's how it is in your case even now. God is knitting together places that were once broken. He's making you stronger than ever. What a gift these scars will become if you view them through His eyes.

Lord, I haven't looked at my physical (or emotional) scars as
a gift until now. I see that You've done a mighty work in my
body and in my heart, seaming me back together and growing
me into a woman of strength. Thank You for such
hard work on my behalf, Lord. Amen.

284

Self-Discipline

For we do not have a high priest who is unable to empathize with our weaknesses, but we have one who has been tempted in every way, just as we are—yet he did not sin.
HEBREWS 4:15 NIV

No one has to tell you to do it. You're self-motivated, driven, full of zeal. And you're committed to the task too. You'll follow through not because others are watching but because you promised yourself you would. "Finish what you start" is your motto. Your daily discipline doesn't go unnoticed by friends and family members, but this isn't about them. You're working hard—at school, job, exercise, and so on—because you want to be the best possible you. Self-discipline is a gift, one you give yourself. By doing so, you're setting an example for others so that they might take up the torch of self-discipline as well.

Lord, thank You for showing me that discipline can be a good thing. It keeps me moving forward, making progress. It gives me boundaries. Best of all, it's a gift I can give myself. I'm excited to see what the future looks like, Father. Give me the tenacity to keep going, I pray. Amen.

Majestic Mountain Peaks

*How beautiful upon the mountains are the feet of him
who brings good news, who publishes peace, who brings
good news of happiness, who publishes salvation,
who says to Zion, "Your God reigns."*
ISAIAH 52:7 ESV

They rise before you, their snowy tops almost kissing the sky.
These majestic mountain peaks seem to point straight to heaven
as if to say, "Look who created us!" You can almost picture the
Lord using His fingertip to pull each one up from the earth's
crust. When you're in the mountains, you witness nature at its
finest. You experience higher heights, greater vision, expanded
perspective. Isn't that just how God wants us to live, in the
mountaintops with Him? We can see through His eyes, hear
through His ears, and impact a world in need of love.

*Lord, my heart is at home in the mountains. In that lofty
place, I almost feel like I can reach up and touch You.
You're as near as my next breath. Thank You for reminding
me that You've called me to live with higher vision, Lord,
to see and hear as You do so that I can affect change
in my world. I long to do just that. Amen.*

Kindness

A man who is kind benefits himself,
but a cruel man hurts himself.
PROVERBS 11:17 ESV

Don't you love kind people? They are considerate, generous, always looking out for the other guy. It's great to be on the receiving end, but it's also fun to give it away. Kindness is a gift you can offer those around you even when they don't deserve it. In fact, unconditional kindness can win over even the toughest critic. Best of all, kindness is good for your health. It causes you to calm down and think before you act. It can lower blood pressure, soothe a pounding headache, and calm your racing heart. Quite a lovely medicine, kindness. So receive it... and offer it. You will benefit yourself and those around you with this beautiful gift.

Lord, show me those in my path who need my kindness
today. I want to extend this gift as an offering so others can
be blessed as so many have blessed me. Guard my heart,
Father, that my reactions and responses to others
will be seen as kind not callous. Amen.

Church

"And I tell you, you are Peter, and on this rock I will build my church, and the gates of hell shall not prevail against it."
MATTHEW 16:18 ESV

It's more than just steeples and bells, choir lofts and pews. It's more than a contemporary worship service, an excellent sermon, and a cool coffee bar. The Church is the convergence of people of every race, every tribe, every tongue, all coming together as one in Jesus' name. In this amazing family, all are welcome regardless of background. The Church is a representation of the Lord on this earth and is one of the finest gifts God offers to a watching world. You're part of that gift, an important member. The world is watching, and they want to know how they can experience the sense of unity you have. And so you invite them in. They come at your bidding and before long walk joyfully into a relationship with the King of kings and become part of the body too. Isn't it amazing to know that you can play a role in all of that? The Church is a gift. . .and so are you.

Father, thank You for the reminder that I am the Church.
I'm part of the family. I want to reach others with Your love,
Lord. Teach me how to love as only the body of Christ can.
Praise You in advance for the work You are doing
all across this planet, Father. Amen.

Pastors

" 'And I will give you shepherds after my own heart,
who will feed you with knowledge and understanding.' "
JEREMIAH 3:15 ESV

They give their lives in service to their congregations, often overlooking their personal needs to care for others. They work countless hours, rushing from church to hospitals and homes of parishioners. Pastors shepherd the flock as only they know how to do. Their compassion reaches far and wide. You love the man of God who shepherds your church. He stands before you on Sunday morning and pours out every word the Lord has laid on his heart. He preps lessons for the following week and then begins the whole process all over again. He's such a gift to the body, and you want to bless him, but what can you do? How about taking up a special offering to send him off on a little vacation with his wife? Maybe an unexpected cruise or road trip? The possibilities are endless, and he's worth it!

Father, I'm grateful for my pastor. He works so hard on our
behalf. Bless him, I pray. Meet every need, financial
and otherwise. Guard and protect his family,
and bring peace and joy, I pray. Amen.

289

Consistency

Whatever you do, work at it with all your heart,
as working for the Lord, not for human masters.
COLOSSIANS 3:23 NIV

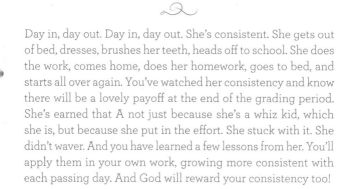

Day in, day out. Day in, day out. She's consistent. She gets out
of bed, dresses, brushes her teeth, heads off to school. She does
the work, comes home, does her homework, goes to bed, and
starts all over again. You've watched her consistency and know
there will be a lovely payoff at the end of the grading period.
She's earned that A not just because she's a whiz kid, which
she is, but because she put in the effort. She stuck with it. She
didn't waver. And you have learned a few lessons from her. You'll
apply them in your own work, growing more consistent with
each passing day. And God will reward your consistency too!

* * *

Lord, I love consistent people. No wishy-washiness. They do
what needs to be done, usually without prompting, and keep
their eyes on the prize. I want to be like that too, Father,
so help me maintain consistency in all I do. Amen.

Diversity

As a prisoner for the Lord, then, I urge you to live a life worthy of the calling you have received. Be completely humble and gentle; be patient, bearing with one another in love. Make every effort to keep the unity of the Spirit through the bond of peace.
EPHESIANS 4:1–3 NIV

They're all different. Different colors. Different sizes. Different shapes. Different personalities. They have unique perspectives, opposing viewpoints when it comes to politics, and even varying ideas on how people should dress, speak, and wear their hair. These are your friends and loved ones in the body of Christ. Many sit right across the aisle from you on a typical Sunday morning. There in that sanctuary, you don't see differences; you see similarities. This person wants to win others to Christ just like you do. That one is hoping to raise her children to love Jesus. You have the same goal. The truth is, you have much more in common than things that are different. So celebrate the diversity. How boring would it be if we were all the same, anyway?

Lord, I'm grateful for diversity. My brothers and sisters sharpen me, challenge my thinking, and cause me to grow. Though we're all different, bond us as one, I pray, Lord. Amen.

Teamwork

How good and pleasant it is when
God's people live together in unity!
PSALM 133:1 NIV

All for one and one for all. That's how you are around your team, your circle of friends. You perform at your best when you're together. You know each other's weaknesses and strengths. One knows how to pick up the slack when the other is off her game. Together, you've done amazing things—pulled off women's events, run bake sales, worked deals for your company, sold products, produced amazing meals. You've raised money for charities, planned weddings, and even managed a baby shower or two. What one could never do alone, you pulled off as a pack. And what a gift this pack is. You wouldn't trade in one member. Instead, you stick together, for there's power in numbers.

Lord, I love teamwork. There's something so exciting about
pulling off a big event with a group of friends, coworkers,
or loved ones. Thanks for placing strong people around me,
Father. Together, we're invincible. Sure, we work hard, but it's
worth it. I'm so grateful for every single person, Lord! Amen.

292

Serving

*Each of you should use whatever gift you have received
to serve others, as faithful stewards of God's
grace in its various forms.*
1 PETER 4:10 NIV

God created you to serve. Whether you give of time, talents, or treasures, He wants you to pour yourself out as an offering so that others will be blessed. (He'll bless you in return when you live this sort of life.) So whom will you serve? Your aging parents? Your child's teacher? An elderly neighbor? A friend who's just had surgery? The women's ministry at your church? The children's pastor? The choir director? Ask the Lord to show you how and where to give your time. And don't be surprised if God takes you out of your comfort zone. He's good at that. You might just find yourself feeding the homeless, traveling to a foreign country on a mission trip, or leading worship at a nearby retirement center. God has great things in mind if you'll just allow Him to nudge you out of the box.

*Lord, it's a little frightening, I confess, to put myself out there,
to say "I'll serve." I'm not sure where You'll take me, Father,
but I know I can trust You. So I put my hand
in Yours today, Lord. Amen.*

Giving

"In all things I have shown you that by working hard in this way we must help the weak and remember the words of the Lord Jesus, how he himself said, 'It is more blessed to give than to receive.'"
ACTS 20:35 ESV

Perhaps you've heard the old adage "It's better to give than to receive." Why do you suppose that is? Receiving is pretty fun, after all. Truth is, you're created in the image of God, and He's a giver. He gave us life. He gave His Son. He sent the Holy Spirit. He continues to pour out blessings day after day. And He wants you to emulate that behavior. So make up your mind—be known as a giver. Let your generosity lead the way. Tend to those in need. Give to your church. Donate to a favorite charity. Sponsor a child overseas. Do whatever the Lord leads you to do. When you give from a generous heart, you're not just blessing others; that blessing boomerangs back to you. Sounds like fun, doesn't it?

Father, I love to give—whether I'm putting money in the offering plate at church or paying for the uniforms of a Little League team. Whether I'm buying coffee for the man behind me in line at the coffee shop or baking cookies for a neighbor. May I always have a giving spirit, Lord. There's such joy in blessing others. Give me creative ideas, I pray. Amen.

294

Bravery

I lift up my eyes to the hills. From where does my help come?
My help comes from the LORD, who made heaven and earth.
He will not let your foot be moved; he who keeps you will
not slumber. Behold, he who keeps Israel will neither
slumber nor sleep. The LORD is your keeper;
theLORD is your shade on your right hand.
PSALM 121:1–5 ESV

You've watched enough movies to know what bravery looks like. On the big screen, the timid one reluctantly takes her bow and arrow and faces her enemy head-on. Because of the lessons she's learned on her journey, she wins the battle. The same is true in your life. If you can face your enemies head-on (as little David did with the giant, Goliath), then God will reward your courage. He'll fight the battle on your behalf. People will stand in awe, wondering how you managed such a feat, but you'll know the truth—it was really God, stepping up and rewarding your bravery. What's holding you back today? What are you afraid of? Look that enemy in the eye, summon up your courage, and grab that bow and arrow!

Lord, my courage fades at times. I don't feel brave.
But I want to be a mighty warrior for You. Give me
courage to stand and then fight that battle, I pray. Amen.

A Supportive Church

And they devoted themselves to the apostles' teaching and the fellowship, to the breaking of bread and the prayers.
ACTS 2:42 ESV

You're really going through it. Your husband's lost his job. Just buying groceries is tough. Then one morning you open your front door to discover someone has left several bags of groceries on your front porch. The following Sunday a friend from church slips a card in your purse with money inside. You get a call from the prayer team. They've added your family to the list and want to know if there's anything the church can do. Having a supportive church is important, especially when you're going through a tough season. Knowing that others are praying and that they have your back really serves as a necessary boost when you're down. Today, thank the Lord for your church body. If you haven't been involved in a church, start searching for one. The body of Christ will be there for you, and it will feel mighty good when you're able to be there for them as well.

What a gift, Lord! My church is the best. No matter what roads I walk down, they are there to hold my hand. They help in times of need, offer love and encouragement when I'm facing new opportunities, and pray without ceasing. I'm not sure what I did to deserve them, but I'm grateful, Father. Amen.

Hot Coffee

So, whether you eat or drink, or whatever you do,
do all to the glory of God.
1 CORINTHIANS 10:31 ESV

You smell it when you walk past the coffee shop at the mall. Its scent draws you in like a magnet tugging at you until you just can't help yourself. You have to have a cup of that steaming hot brew. So you cross over the threshold and step inside to discover a dozen or more people who've already purchased their cups of coffee. They're seated at small tables, some reading newspapers, others working on laptops, and others chatting with friends. You'll soon join them. Coffee has that power. It calms you when you need calming, wakes you when you need waking, and brings a smile to your face when you're down in the dumps. It warms you on a cold day, brings a flood of memories as you enjoy that first sip, and offers comfort that few things can. You love it, and that will never change.

Lord, I'm grateful for all the things you provide, but I'm especially grateful for coffee. It's more than an elixir on days when I'm feeling blue; it's a little bit of heaven in a cup. There will be coffee in heaven. Right, Lord? Amen.

Cozy Blankets

In peace I will both lie down and sleep; for you alone,
O LORD, make me dwell in safety.
PSALM 4:8 ESV

You have your favorite. It's worn and soft, even has a tiny hole or two in it. But you wouldn't trade it for anything in the world. That blanket is your friend. You're like Linus from the Peanuts gang, unwilling to let it go. And why would you? It's a part of the fiber of your being, a gift, a cozy "everything's gonna be okay" wrapper. Doesn't it feel good to have that one special blanket that means something to you? Maybe it's a quilt your grandmother made. Maybe it's a blanket passed down from a great-aunt. Maybe it's something you picked out years ago and still love to this day. For whatever reason, it has planted itself in your heart, and you've made up your mind you won't let go even if it is worn and frazzled.

Lord, I feel Your love cocooning me just like that special
blanket. I feel so safe with You, Lord. Thank You for the
reminder that You want to bring feelings of
comfort, Father. I'm grateful. Amen.

BFFs

*As soon as he had finished speaking to Saul, the soul
of Jonathan was knit to the soul of David,
and Jonathan loved him as his own soul.*
1 SAMUEL 18:1 ESV

We used to call them best friends. These days, they've been labeled BFFs (Best Friends Forever). Regardless of what you call your closest friend, she's the one who knows you best. She can tell when you're struggling and when you're sailing. She's there when you're heartbroken and is the first one in line to bring a meal if you're down for the count. This concept of a best friend dates back to the Old Testament to the story of David and Jonathan, who were friends as close as brothers. The kindred spirit between these two has inspired millions and shown us that God puts His stamp of approval on deep friendships. Who is the one your soul is knit to? Who do you love like a sister? Today, thank God for the gift that this special friend has been in your life.

*Lord, I'm grateful for all of my friends. There are so many
special ones in the pack. Some I'm closer to than others,
and a few are like sisters to me, but I'm especially touched by
the deep friendships You've provided over the years.
What a gift, Father. I'm extremely grateful. Amen.*

Pushy People

Therefore confess your sins to each other and pray for each other so that you may be healed. The prayer of a righteous person is powerful and effective.
JAMES 5:16 NIV

Sometimes she gets on your nerves. She's always telling you how you could've done better at this or that. She has big plans for you, for your projects. And you do your best not to get annoyed when her enthusiasm plows you down, because this woman—your parent, spouse, daughter, neighbor, pastor's wife, friend, boss, coworker—is nudging you to become a more excellent version of yourself. Okay, it doesn't always feel like it in the moment, but you can choose to take her words and apply the ones that are meant to stick then discard the rest. Truthfully, pushy people are hard to get along with for the most part, but you've drawn your boundaries and know how to stick to your guns when you need to. Through the actions of this woman, you're growing into a stronger person sometimes by applying what she's sharing, other times by learning how to say no.

Lord, I'll admit it's been hard to deal with some of the pushy people in my life. Today I make a conscious choice to use those situations, those relationships, to grow stronger both as a woman and in my faith. Amen.

300

The Freedom to Be Yourself

But let each one test his own work, and then his reason to boast will be in himself alone and not in his neighbor.
GALATIANS 6:4 ESV

There's no putting on airs around this friend. You don't even have to wear makeup if you don't want to. She gives you the freedom to be yourself. You don't need to come up with grand stories to impress her or buy expensive clothing to keep up with her. She's a kindred spirit who happens to love you just the way you are. And you love her too. When you're together, you're both relaxed at home. If the house is a little messy, who cares? If the laundry needs folding, she helps you. She encourages you to grow into the woman of God you're called to be. You don't have to fit into someone else's image. Don't you just love these friends? They make it so easy to be yourself, to be comfortable, to make mistakes (and even corrections) in their presence. Today, while you're thanking God for these amazing friends, make up your mind to be an amazing friend to someone else. Somewhere out there, there's a woman who just wants someone to tell her, "It's okay to be yourself."

I want to be that kind of friend, Father, the kind who says, "Hey, just relax! Be yourself around me." Lead me to those who need that kind of love, Lord. Amen.

301

Recliners

"For I will satisfy the weary soul,
and every languishing soul I will replenish."
JEREMIAH 31:25 ESV

They might not be the prettiest pieces of furniture in the house, but recliners serve their purpose. They elevate tired feet, provide comfort after a long day's work, and even provide a place to sleep after surgery. Recliners reduce stress, help with circulation, and are particularly helpful when you're expecting. They can reduce swelling in feet, help with your center of gravity, and relieve aching joints. In short, these chairs are a gift. Today, as you kick back and put up your feet, take the time to thank God for seasons of rest and reflection. You don't have to go to a mountain stream or a sandy beach to find a place of rest. Just lean back in your own recliner and enjoy several moments of rest.

Father, thank You for giving me a place to rest and relax
in my own home. With all of the stresses of life, I'm so
happy for a place to call my own. Feet up, Lord!
I have some resting to do. Amen.

302

Work Ethic

But those who hope in the Lord will renew their strength.
They will soar on wings like eagles; they will run and
not grow weary, they will walk and not be faint.
ISAIAH 40:31 NIV

Don't you appreciate people with a good work ethic? They are a real blessing both to their bosses and the companies (or groups) they represent. Someone with a strong work ethic won't give up on a job only halfway done. She sees it through to the end, no matter how difficult. She's not swayed by people who want to distract her either. She knows when to play and when to work. Pause for a moment to think about the people in your world who have a strong work ethic. What do you find admirable about them? What would you like to glean from their lives? Ask God to show you what it means to have a good work ethic, one that propels you to do great things. What a gift this strong work ethic can be. It benefits everyone.

Father, thank You for those who work so hard. They do not go unnoticed, Lord. I admire them so much. May they inspire me to work harder, soar higher, accomplish more for You. Amen.

303

PJs

And he said to them, "Come away by yourselves to a desolate place and rest a while." For many were coming and going, and they had no leisure even to eat.
MARK 6:31 ESV

They're worn. They're faded. They're soft. They bring comfort like nothing else can. They're your PJs, and you wouldn't trade them for anything in the world. PJs are like an old friend—the moment you start thinking about them, the better you feel. And when you slide them on, every care, every trouble, vanishes. They've seen you through the flu, a broken ankle, and recovery after surgery. They're frayed from your washer, stained because of that time you ate dinner in them, and ripped across the knee. But you don't care. They are your friends and will remain with you until someone forcibly removes them from your home. PJs are a gift, one you wouldn't trade for anything.

Lord, there's something so comfortable about slipping into PJs. From the minute they go on, I feel better. I love the feeling I get when I'm lounging, Father, and I'm grateful for the perfect clothing to lounge in. Amen.

304

Home-Cooked Meals

Every moving thing that lives shall be food for you. And as I gave you the green plants, I give you everything.
GENESIS 9:3 ESV

Nothing can compare to a good, home-cooked meal. You can't emulate it in a restaurant—you certainly won't experience the same pleasure you'll receive at your own table. Whether it's Mama's chicken and dumplings, your sweetheart's chili, or your neighbor's burgers, home-cooked food just makes your day better, warms your heart, and comforts you. So what's your favorite home-cooked food? Maybe it's time to head to the grocery store to buy the ingredients so you can bless your loved ones with a meal they won't soon forget. Chances are, one day those kids of yours will pass on your recipes to their children and grandchildren. Home-cooked meals are a gift that keeps giving and giving, from generation to generation.

Lord, I'm grateful for my mother and her mother before her for writing down recipes or passing down family dishes. Help me keep the old traditions alive, Father, by writing down the recipes so they can be enjoyed for years to come. Amen.

305

Freedom of Speech

Live as people who are free, not using your freedom as a
cover-up for evil, but living as servants of God.
1 PETER 2:16 ESV

You're free to tell others what you believe. And so you do. They might not agree, but that's okay. They're free to express their opinions too. One of our greatest blessings is the freedom to share in this way. Sure, things can get messy, especially if people press their opinion with too much force, but freedom of speech has always come at a cost. So don't be afraid to share. Use wisdom when you do, of course, but don't hide your light under a bushel. Freedom of speech is a gift. We don't know how long we'll have it, so follow the lead of the Holy Spirit and speak out on issues that matter to you while you can. And while you're at it, pray for those in authority over you that they might continue to see this freedom as a forever gift, one that can't be taken away.

Father, I get nervous when I see our freedoms slipping away.
Sometimes it's hard to share my faith or even my opinions
without fear of repercussion. Please show me how I can speak
my heart without adding to the turmoil, Lord. I want to be
a good witness for You, but I don't want to hurt
others along the way. Help me, I pray. Amen.

Political Leaders

Jesus said to them, "Render to Caesar the things
that are Caesar's, and to God the things that
are God's." And they marveled at him.
MARK 12:17 ESV

From the president all the way down to your city councilpersons, you are represented by a host of politicians. They vote at the community, county, state, and national levels on things that matter to you. Some of them are in your corner; others have opposing views. These men and women—the ones with whom you agree and the ones you don't—are civil servants, representatives, gifts. They speak for the people. They're listening closely t what you have to say. These fine people need our prayers so they can do the best possible job. Today, pause to think about your representatives. List them on a piece of paper, and then put it on your refrigerator. Lift them up in prayer as often as you can. Ask God to open their ears and their hearts not just to the will of the people but to God's ultimate will as well.

Father, I'm so grateful for my representatives. May You guide
and protect each one. Be with their families, their coworkers,
and the ones they represent, Lord. Speak words of truth
to each one so that they can vote according
to Your will, Father. Amen.

307

Gratitude

Give thanks to the Lord, for he is good,
for his steadfast love endures forever.
PSALM 136:1 ESV

Don't you love people who show gratitude when you perform an act of kindness? Maybe you cook a scrumptious meal and then wonder if anyone even noticed the time you put into it. One of the kids returns to the kitchen to say, "Thanks, Mom. That was great." Or maybe you put in extra hours at work, thinking no one is watching. Then, randomly, your boss passes by your desk and smiles. "I saw how hard you worked on that project. Great job." There's something about words of gratitude to stir you to action. You can keep going as long as those you're helping are thankful. The same is true in reverse. Right now people are working on your behalf. When was the last time you showed gratitude? This might be the perfect day for that.

* * *

Father, may I never forget to be grateful. I know how much
it means to hear those simple words: "Thank you" or "You've
done a great job." Those words make everything
worth it. Thank You for grateful people, Lord.
May I be one of them, I pray. Amen.

308

Honesty

*Better is a poor person who walks in his integrity than
one who is crooked in speech and is a fool.*
PROVERBS 19:1 ESV

Not everyone in this world is honest. Some people can't be
trusted at all. That's why it's important to be who you say you
are and do what you say you'll do. Honesty is a gift you give
others. The Bible says that lying lips are an abomination to the
Lord. He's hurt by dishonesty as much or more than your friends
and loved ones. Sure, there will be times when you wish you
could tell a little white lie. It might seem easier to be dishonest.
But God calls for total purity from His kids. It's true what they
say: honesty really is the best policy. So give the gift of honesty.
And if you're spending too much time with a dishonest person,
maybe it's time to ease out of the relationship at least for the
time being. No point in remaining on the receiving end of a
deceitful friend.

*Honesty really is the best policy, Lord. You've called me to be
truthful in all my dealings. Help me as I work with others
who are not so honest. Give me the ability to tell the
truth from a lie so I can be protected from any
evil schemes. Guard me, I pray. Amen.*

309

Compassion

And Saul said, "May you be blessed by the LORD,
for you have had compassion on me."
1 SAMUEL 23:21 ESV

To fully understand the word *compassion*, you need to break it down. The prefix (com-) means "with" or "for." When you have compassion for others, you're "with" passion "for" others. The world is full of passionate people, but many are self-serving, passionate about their own dreams, ideologies, goals, etc. There's nothing wrong with any of that, but when you find someone who's passionate about others, you've really found a gift. What about you? Are you surrounded by compassionate people who seem to be with/for you? Take the time to thank God for them today. And would others say that you are compassionate? If not, then ask the Lord to show you how to become more focused on others.

Thank You, Lord, for the many compassionate people in my
life. They've been there for me during the hard times
and are with me still. May I learn this kind of compassion,
Father, so that I can reach out with Your love
and care to others in need. Amen.

310

Courage

And Joshua said to them, "Do not be afraid or dismayed;
be strong and courageous. For thus the Lord will do
to all your enemies against whom you fight."
JOSHUA 10:25 ESV

Squared shoulders. Determination. Bravery. You have a difficult task before you, and you're ready. You've steeled your resolve and prayed for courage. Now it's time to head straight into the heat of the battle. You would sooner do anything else, but here you are, doing what needs to be done. And you're not afraid. Yesterday your knees were knocking, your voice was quivering, and your belly was filled with butterflies. But something happened after your most recent chat with God. Now you feel invincible. Hopeful. You're not angry. You're not out for revenge. You're just ready. And bravery leads the way as you clothe yourself in the weapons of warfare God has given you. Deep breath. You're headed in.

Lord, my courage wanes at times. That's when I really count
on You to come through for me. I'm David, fighting the mighty
Goliath. But I know who wins in the end, and that
bolsters my courage, Father. Keep me strong
from the inside out, I pray. Amen.

311

Thanksgiving

Enter his gates with thanksgiving, and his courts with praise!
Give thanks to him; bless his name!
PSALM 100:4 ESV

Don't you just love Thanksgiving? Having a special day to express thanks for the people, places, and things in your life is a gift. Thanksgiving prompts us to look at everyone around us—brothers, sisters, parents, children, friends—and realize what a gift they are. It takes a simple meal—turkey, stuffing, potatoes, and so on—and turns it into a feast, a visible reminder that the "little" things in our lives are really our sustenance, our joy. What are you grateful for this Thanksgiving? Who has outdone herself showing you love this past year? What special event stands out to you as the biggest blessing since last Thanksgiving? Remember to thank God for all these things and more. When we pause to acknowledge, we're blessing God's heart. And don't forget...someone somewhere is thanking God for you today. You are loved.

Father, I'm so grateful for the many ways You've blessed me.
You've surrounded me with amazing people. You've met my
needs and then some. You've blessed me with health
and comfort. How I praise You, Lord. Amen.

312

Falling Leaves

*All the host of heaven shall rot away, and the skies roll
up like a scroll. All their host shall fall, as leaves fall
from the vine, like leaves falling from the fig tree.*
ISAIAH 34:4 ESV

It clings tightly to the branches, unrelenting in its quest. To let
go would be to admit defeat. Then, as autumn's winds begin
to blow, transformation occurs. Once green, the leaf morphs
to yellow then red then brown. Now dry and brittle, it can hold
on no more. In defeat, it releases its hold on the branch and
drifts slowly to the ground below, joining hundreds of others in
the pile in the yard. One season has ended. Another one is on
the way. Perhaps you know what that feels like. Maybe you're
feeling a bit unusable like those leaves. Don't despair. You may
find yourself dry and brittle today, but a new season is coming.
God still has many things in your future. So look at those falling
leaves as a gift, a symbol of the Lord's amazing plan.

*My best days are ahead of me, Lord. I truly believe that.
Yes, I've been through seasons of change, but that doesn't
mean my usefulness is behind me. I have big things
ahead, Father. Thank You for that reminder. Amen.*

343

Fuel

"Therefore, thus says the Lord GOD, 'As the wood of the vine among the trees of the forest, which I have given to the fire for fuel, so have I given up the inhabitants of Jerusalem.'"
EZEKIEL 15:6 NASB

It keeps your car running, your lawn mower ready to do battle with blades of grass, and even keeps your body alive and well. Fuel is what makes us go. For the car and mower, it's gasoline. For your body, it's food—grains, vegetables, proteins, and so on. Without fuel, planes couldn't fly, puppies wouldn't grow into dogs, yards would wither and die, and city busses would sit empty and still. Without fuel, you couldn't run your heater. Fuel (food) is critical to the upward motion of societies all across the globe. And God provides it. Through this amazing planet, He's given us what we need to fuel our homes, vehicles, other modes of transportation, and even our bodies. He thought of everything, didn't He? What an amazing God He is.

Lord, it's remarkable to think about how many man-made items need fuel (something You created long in advance of our man-made items) to run. Amazing! You knew we would need these things and provided for our needs ahead of time. How kind You are, Father. Amen.

314

Grace

I became a servant of this gospel by the gift of God's grace given me through the working of his power.
EPHESIANS 3:7 NIV

Perhaps you've seen the acronym: G.R.A.C.E.—God's Riches at Christ's Expense. Grace is that intangible thing we receive from God that we really don't deserve. You could look at it as a combination of mercy, favor, forgiveness, and so many other positive, uplifting things He places on a silver platter and passes our way. We did nothing to earn grace, nor can we lose it. It's one of the most amazing gifts God offers His kids. It's also something He longs for us to give others. When we've been wronged. When our feelings are hurt. When someone inadvertently causes us pain. Instead of reacting with anger or irritation, we could and should pass that silver platter from our hands to the one who's injured us. Today, spend time thanking God for this amazing gift.

Lord, I'm so grateful for Your grace. It was and is undeserved, Father. In fact, after all the mistakes I've made, I don't qualify for it based on my actions. But You're not keeping score, Lord. You've decided to bless me with this gift—Your riches—even at my lowest point. Today I commit to extending it to others as You have blessed me. Amen.

315

Food

And God said, "Behold, I have given you every plant yielding seed that is on the face of all the earth, and every tree with seed in its fruit. You shall have them for food."
GENESIS 1:29 ESV

Have you ever thought about what life would be like without food? No fresh fruit. No cheeseburgers. No chicken salad. No bread. No dessert. God could have created us with no need for food whatsoever. How sad would that be? Instead, He created us with a daily need. Not a want but a bona fide need. If not for food, we wouldn't survive. As you ponder that reality, why not pause to thank God for the food He provides not just on a daily basis but from year to year. He kept you fed as a child and has plenty more where that came from now that you're older. He knows your likes and dislikes and has all sorts of food surprises headed your way. What a gift, that yummy food!

Father, thank You for designing me to need food for my survival. I can't imagine what life would be like if I didn't pause two or three times a day not just to consume protein, starches, and vegetables but to spend time with those I love. Table fellowship is the best, Lord. I'm so grateful You came up with this plan. Amen.

316

Table Set for Guests

"For where two or three gather in my name,
there am I with them."
MATTHEW 18:20 NIV

You spend quality time making everything look perfect. The centerpiece—a gorgeous number you put together yourself—grounds the table. Everything else is in place—a lovely tablecloth, your best plates, silverware, cloth napkins. Glasses are filled with ice, and the luscious smell of food wafts from the kitchen. You give the table one last glance, deciding a couple candles are in order. You locate them, place them on either side of the centerpiece, and then reach for some matches to light them. There. That's perfect. You're tempted to take a picture of the table, but the doorbell rings. It's time to welcome your guests. And that's what this is all about, after all, those special people who make your heart smile. They're worth all of this—the hours prepping the meal and the added work making your table look perfect. You greet them with a smile, and the party's on!

Lord, thank You for special events that call for a lovely table.
I have so much fun putting everything together. In fact, I get
great pleasure out of making things look lovely. Thank You for
the gift of special meals with those I love, Father. Amen.

Online Shopping

*Consider the ravens: they neither sow nor reap, they have
neither storehouse nor barn, and yet God feeds them.
Of how much more value are you than the birds!*
LUKE 12:24 ESV

Oh, the ease of online shopping! You can make your selections,
purchase them, and receive confirmation all at the push of a
button. Two to three days later, the items are on your front
doorstep, waiting for you. Best of all, you don't have to go anywhere. . .you can shop in your PJs, no makeup required! The
ability to purchase goods without leaving your home is a gift,
one your parents and grandparents didn't have. Online shopping is especially helpful during the Christmas season, when
the malls are jam-packed with customers, or when you're not
feeling well and can't leave home. It's also a great option for
those who aren't keen on the shopping experience as a whole.
No matter how you look at it, online shopping is a win-win.

*Lord, maybe I'm a little spoiled, but I love shopping online.
I don't have to get dressed up or put wear and tear on my car.
I don't need to drag all of the kids out or find someone
to watch them. With the click of a button, I can make
my purchase and get on with my day. I'm so
grateful for that option! Amen.*

318

Mediators

For there is one God, and there is one mediator
between God and men, the man Christ Jesus.
1 TIMOTHY 2:5 ESV

They stand in the gap for you, ready to do battle on your behalf. They're lawyers, counselors, therapists, parents, pastors, teachers, friends—and they care enough to get involved. In fact, they go a step further and speak for you. These people are such a gift, particularly when you find yourself in a place of need. Of course, there's no greater mediator than Jesus Himself. He bridged the gap between heaven and earth. He came to bridge the two so you could have eternal life. Like those great mediators you know, He cared enough to speak on your behalf. When He said, "It is finished," on the cross that infamous day, He was speaking for you. You no longer need to try to earn your way to heaven. He's done the intermediary work for you. What an amazing counselor and friend!

Father, thank You for sending Jesus to be my mediator.
I couldn't ask for a better representative. I love the words
He speaks over me. For all the wonderful mediators
in my life, I'm so thankful, Lord. Amen.

Adoption

He predestined us for adoption to himself as sons through
Jesus Christ, according to the purpose of his will.
EPHESIANS 1:5 ESV

People pass by her and whisper, "She's not really their child. They adopted her." You're tempted to stop in your tracks and correct them, but you release a slow breath and calm down. They don't get it. She's a child of your heart, a true gift from heaven. And though the process was difficult, you would do it all over again just to end up with this precious child. Adoption is more than a process of bringing a stranger into your home; it's the act of sweeping someone into the fold, bringing that child into the family. She is your daughter. She will always be your daughter. And whether the world understands or not, the process of bringing her into the family is one you cherish.

Father, even if others don't understand, I do. You've grafted
this child into my heart just as You grafted me into Your
great family. I'm so grateful for the process of adoption, Lord.
May every orphaned child find a loving family, I pray. Amen.

320

Integrity

Whoever walks in integrity walks securely,
but he who makes his ways crooked will be found out.
PROVERBS 10:9 ESV

Morally upright. Principled. Honest. Whole. Undivided. Walking the straight and narrow. These words describe an individual of integrity. He's not popping up as a breaking story on the six o'clock news. She's not the one others are worrying about. People of integrity really are who they say they are. They're a gift to society. That's why the scripture from Proverbs says that a person of integrity walks securely. No tipping to the right or left. No swaying back and forth. Integrity is a gift you give yourself, one that ends up spilling over onto others. So how would you describe yourself? Are you a woman of integrity? Are you undivided? Upright? Do you do the things you say you'll do, refrain from the things you shouldn't touch? A woman of integrity will go a long way in this life as she represents Christ in all she does.

Lord, I want to represent You as a woman of great integrity.
When others see me, I don't ever want them to wonder
if I'm principled, upright. Let my character shine
through as I live for You, Father. Amen.

324

Loyalty

And David said, "I will deal loyally with Hanun the son of Nahash, as his father dealt loyally with me." So David sent by his servants to console him concerning his father. And David's servants came into the land of the Ammonites.
2 SAMUEL 10:2 ESV

There are those who stick closer than family. You don't have to invite them over. They know when to come. You don't have to ask for help. They're already there, helping. You don't need their counsel, their love. They've already offered it. These loyal friends are worth their weight in gold. And when it comes to dealing with you—in the marketplace, church, or elsewhere—they extend the same hand of loyalty. You're kin, though not of the same mother or father. This sort of loyalty is a gift, one you couldn't buy for all the money in the world, and it's a gift you won't take for granted. You'll offer the same sort of loyalty in return. After all, that's what friendship is all about. What a gift loyal friends are!

Father, I'm so grateful for the friends who stick with me no matter what I'm going through. They're my defenders, my coaches, my friends. They're loyal to a fault. May I be that kind of friend in return, I pray. Amen.

322

Responsibility

*May the Lord direct your hearts to the love of
God and to the steadfastness of Christ.*
2 THESSALONIANS 3:5 ESV

Responsible people are a gift, a breath of fresh air. You don't
have to remind them. You don't have to wonder if they'll skip
out on you. You don't have to nudge them to get the job done.
They're already two steps ahead of you with the task at hand
and encouraging others to do the same. They lead by example
and others follow willingly, hoping to glean from the masters.
God longs for His kids to be responsible, steadfast, consistent.
This is part of the believer's testimony, after all, setting a great
example. Doing the right thing doesn't always come easily, but
it's always right. Today, offer the gift of responsibility to your
coworkers, your family, your neighborhood, and your community. It's a gift that keeps on giving.

*Father, may I be known as one who is responsible in word and
deed. I want to be a person of my word, someone who follows
through. I don't want to leave people wondering whether
or not I'll do what I've promised. Help me, Lord,
that I might be a good representative of You.
You always carry through, Father! Amen.*

323

Humility

When pride comes, then comes disgrace,
but with humility comes wisdom.
PROVERBS 11:2 NIV

Submitting yourself to the authority of others is difficult, particularly if that person relishes in humbling you. Isn't it comforting to know that, when you humble yourself in the sight of the Lord, He will lift you up? It's not easy to walk in humility, especially if you are trying to prove your self-worth or value, but God is the best exalter. So how do you feel about humility in light of your current situations? Are you feeling you've been humbled too much by someone? If so, it might be time for a tough conversation. Are you, perhaps, squashing someone else, causing them to feel overly humbled? Perhaps some correction is due in that area as well. Humility is great as long as it's in balance. But never be afraid to humble yourself when the situation truly calls for it. You will gain wisdom when you do.

Lord, today I humble myself in Your sight. I admit that
any value I have comes from You. In and of myself,
I'm nothing. My worth comes from You, Father.
Praise You for that reminder. Amen.

324

Fairness

Open your mouth, judge righteously,
defend the rights of the poor and needy.
PROVERBS 31:9 ESV

Justice. Doing right by others. Playing fair. This is how you want to live. Not everyone will agree with you, of course. People claw and scratch their way to the top of the ladder, not caring whom they trample on the way up. But not you. You're equitable. You're kind. You keep the playing field level for the sake of all involved. And when things get off-kilter for those you love, you defend others who aren't getting a fair shake. Why? Because fairness is a gift, one you're happy to dish out. Maybe you've learned your lessons by watching others do the wrong thing. Life isn't always fair, after all. If it were, then why did Jesus Christ, who never committed a sin, have to die for humankind? The most unfair act of all time resulted in justice for all. Ponder that notion for a while, and then thank Him for such sacrificial love.

Lord, thank You for teaching me, through the actions of
Your Son, what it means to show sacrificial fairness.
I want to be more like You, Father. Show me
daily how I can do just that. Amen.

325

Authenticity

Sanctify them in the truth; your word is truth.
JOHN 17:17 ESV

He's the real deal. You knew it the moment you first saw him in action, helping others. He doesn't say one thing and live another. If the words roll off his lips, he lives them out both in public and at home. There's no doubt in your mind. He won't let folks down. Aren't authentic people a gift? When you're around them, you can put down your guard. There's no secret fear that this friend might stab you in the back or gossip when you're not around. He's proven himself in word and deed. And you want to be like him. His authenticity, his love for the truth, his compassion for others. . .these things make you want to be more authentic too. What a gift authenticity is!

Father, I want to be who I say I am. May my words and my actions match. I don't want people to have to wonder if they're safe with me. Cleanse any places in my heart that don't line up with Your Word, and point me on a path toward total authenticity. Amen.

326

Politeness

Only let your manner of life be worthy of the gospel of Christ, so that whether I come and see you or am absent, I may hear of you that you are standing firm in one spirit, with one mind striving side by side for the faith of the gospel.
PHILIPPIANS 1:27 ESV

Opening the door for others. Nodding and smiling as you pass by. Leaving a generous tip. Assisting someone in need. These are just a few of the ways you can and do extend a hand of politeness. In this rush-about world, people don't always pause to respond politely, but when they do, the payoff is fantastic. Those on the receiving end are wowed by these small acts of kindness. So offer the gift of politeness today. Say "thank you" and "please" when necessary. Treat others with the sort of behavior that is respectful and considerate, the kind that puts them first. And remember, what goes around comes around. Treat others the way you want to be treated, and you'll receive that same treatment in return. That's a promise from the Word of God, one you can count on!

I want to be known as a considerate person, Lord, one who treats others politely. Whenever opportunities present themselves, I want to represent You by exhibiting behaviors that put others first. Show me, moment by moment, how to accomplish this, I pray. Amen.

Inspirational Quotes

*And whatever you do, in word or deed, do everything
in the name of the Lord Jesus, giving thanks
to God the Father through him.*
COLOSSIANS 3:17 ESV

You're feeling a little blue, unable to focus, so you sign on to your favorite social media site and scroll through the newsfeed. Nothing catches your eye until you stumble upon a colorful meme. You pause to read it and find yourself inspired by the quote on it. Suddenly, your mood lifts. A smile tips up the corners of your lips. You find yourself more hopeful. . .all because of a few positive, upbeat words. Isn't it just like God to make sure you're inspired when you need to be? And how fun to be a source of inspiration for others. Today, spend a few minutes looking up a great quote or scripture to post so that others can be inspired. Chances are pretty good you'll be touched too.

*Lord, thank You for those quotes that greet me when I scroll
through my newsfeed. I know they're not there by accident.
May I be a source of inspiration to others as my friends
have been to me. Thanks for the nudge in
that direction, Father. Amen.*

328

Expressions of Gratitude

This is the day that the LORD has made;
let us rejoice and be glad in it.
PSALM 118:24 ESV

A simple thank-you. A bouquet of flowers. An unexpected letter, gushing with sweet words. Don't you love the various ways people show their gratitude? Some can't wait to express it. Others want to level the playing field by returning good deed for good deed. Still others hit the social media airwaves, proclaiming their gratefulness for a particular kindness you've shown them. However you give or receive it, gratitude is a gift. It's one that goes a long way toward cementing relationships and keeping joy alive. So become a pro! Whom do you need to thank today? Is there someone who's gone out of her way to make your life pleasant? Maybe a sweet note is in order. Or even a batch of cookies. Show her your gratitude and keep the chain going.

Father, I am so grateful for the many loving people You've surrounded me with. Please don't ever let me forget what a gift they are. Show me how to express my gratitude in ways that will bless and honor these precious people. Amen.

329

Reconciliation

*All this is from God, who through Christ reconciled us
to himself and gave us the ministry of reconciliation.*
2 CORINTHIANS 5:18 ESV

You thought you'd never speak again. She was hurt. You were
hurt. Silence over months and even years sealed the deal—this
relationship is no more. And then, just when you'd completely
given up, a ray of hope. A shaft of light. A brief conversation in
passing. A phone call. A text. An email. An apology. A recipro-
cated apology. More conversation. Lunch. Tears. Laughter. The
promise of things to come. A hug to add a final "amen" to the
notion that healing has come to this relationship. Aren't you
glad God is in the reconciliation business? He longs for our
broken hearts and relationships to be restored. He can work
even in the most impossible situations. Of course, not every
lost friendship is meant to be restored, but don't give up on
the ones that really matter. Sit back and watch what God does
in His time.

*Father, I trust You. You're a God of reconciliation. You've
reconciled me to You, after all. I give You permission to
restore broken relationships, Lord. Move in Your time
and Your way. Let reconciliation come. Amen.*

330

Logic

Brothers, do not be children in your thinking.
Be infants in evil, but in your thinking be mature.
1 CORINTHIANS 14:20 ESV

The Word of God encourages us to put on our thinking caps, to use our logic. We're told to "reason together," which requires thinking, thinking, thinking. Aren't you glad God has given us brains to use? When life's situations don't make sense to us, we can reason them out and draw conclusions based on His Word and on what the Spirit of God is nudging us to do. We're not to aimlessly follow like sheep led to slaughter. Rather, we're to draw logical conclusions. We're to live as wise children, gleaning from God's Word and moving forward with confidence and courage. We're bolstered by our knowledge that He adores us! How wonderful to be created in the image of a logical Creator.

Thank You for the gift of logic, Father. I love thinking things through. I want to be mature in my thinking, Lord, especially when life's situations don't make sense. Give me Your reasoning abilities, I pray. Amen.

331

Truth

*Lead me in your truth and teach me, for you are the God
of my salvation; for you I wait all the day long.*
PSALM 25:5 ESV

The truth will set you free. That's a promise from the Word of
God. When the enemy rears his ugly head and speaks untruths
about you, wait for truth to split the skies wide open and come
shining through. It will happen in God's time. Don't try to rush
it, or you'll miss the potential to witness a miracle. The Lord
always has a way of bringing truth revelation at the most im-
pactful moment. No matter where you are today—beaten down
by untruths or muddling through confusion due to someone
else's dishonest living—know that God will right what has
been wronged. And in the meantime, be bold about the truth
you speak. Not hateful, just bold. Don't cower or bow down to
those who try to get you to conform to untruthful living. Stand
fast. Be firm. And accept truth as the gift it is.

*Thank You for the reminder, Lord, that You will redeem me
and right all wrongs. Untruths will be revealed. Truth will
shine through. While I'm waiting, help me to be a woman
of truth, unaffected by the world around me. Amen.*

332

Police

*"Blessed are the peacemakers,
for they shall be called sons of God."*
MATTHEW 5:9 ESV

~∾~

They stand guard ready to defend you. They risk their lives stepping directly into dangerous situations. They defend the defenseless, intervene in awkward situations, and give their time sacrificially. Police officers, sheriff's deputies, and constables are a gift. In many instances, they are also heroes. Today, take the time to call out the name of an officer you know personally. Lift him or her in prayer. Ask for God's protection, grace, and mercy. Then why not perform a random act of kindness for the officers in your area? A plateful of cookies, perhaps, or some cupcakes might be nice. Go out of your way to let them know they are appreciated.

Father, what a gift these brave men and women are. I could never do the job they so willingly perform. Keep them safe, I pray. Guard and protect them. Keep them from temptation. Guide their steps. Be with their families, and bring peace in every situation, Lord. Amen.

333

Social Media

*And he said to them, "Go into all the world and
proclaim the gospel to the whole creation."*
MARK 16:15 ESV

～

Most people have a love-hate relationship with social media.
They love it because it's a fun way to stay in touch with friends,
loved ones, and folks from days gone by. They hate it because it
often brings out the worst in people, especially during political
seasons. At its core, social media is a gift. It offers opportunity
to have instant access to missionaries in other countries, friends
who've moved away, or grandchildren in another state. Unlike
our grandparents and great-grandparents, we don't have to
wait for a letter to arrive in the mail to know what our loved
ones across the globe are up to. We can find out right now, at
this very instant, thanks to social media. Sure, you don't want
to spend hours a day scrolling through your newsfeed, but if
you take a peek every now and again, you'll have to admit that
staying in touch is a love gift, one you should use with caution.

*Father, thank You for the opportunity to stay in touch with
those I love. Social media has been a huge help, and I'm
grateful for it. Bless those I love all across this globe,
Lord. Thanks for letting me stay in touch. Amen.*

334

A Clear Head

We destroy arguments and every lofty opinion
raised against the knowledge of God, and take
every thought captive to obey Christ.
2 CORINTHIANS 10:5 ESV

There's an old saying that cool heads will prevail. A cool head is a clear head, one free from turmoil and angst. So if you want to prevail, cool down. Let God clear your thoughts, remove the roller-coaster ride going on between your ears. This requires active participation from you, of course. You have to give your thought-life to the Lord daily. Take every thought captive. Don't let your imagination run wild. Take a stand against thoughts that run contrary to the Word of God. They'll do nothing but drag you down. Stay focused on Him, and your regenerated thoughts will lead to a cool head, calm reactions, and better opportunity to prevail.

Sometimes I just need to stop thinking, Lord. I need to stop
letting my troubling thoughts take over, pulling me to places
I don't need to go. I want to be calm and cool-headed, Father.
I want to prevail. So today I choose to take my thoughts
captive, focusing only on what Your Word says. Amen.

335

Disappointment

Return to your stronghold, O prisoners of hope;
today I declare that I will restore to you double.
ZECHARIAH 9:12 ESV

Facing them is tough. You'd rather turn and run or pretend disappointments didn't exist in your world. But you must face them. Yes, your heart is heavy. Sure, this was a tough blow. But you'll get through this. You've made it through bigger disappointments than this in the past. In many ways, you've grown into the woman you are because of them. If you really stop to think it through, you realize sad, hard times, are a gift because they shape and form you. Imagine how different you'd be if you hadn't walked through those valleys. Would you have morphed into the strong woman of God you've become? Probably not. So don't shy away from disappointments. Ask the Lord to take what the enemy has meant for evil in your life and use it for good. He will do it!

Father, I know You'll use this situation for good. You always
do. I don't know how You always manage to bring joy from
the mourning, but You're an expert, Lord. I give
my disappointments to You and ask that You do
Your perfect work in my life, I pray. Amen.

336

The Past

Say not, "Why were the former days better than these?"
For it is not from wisdom that you ask this.
ECCLESIASTES 7:10 ESV

There's a reason the past is called the past. It has already passed. It's over. Done with. Gone. Behind you. Sure, it might've kicked up a little dust on its way out, but even that is dissipating now. So why look back? Why stir up imaginings of what could have been or should have been? Why give time and energy to something you can't change? The past offers but two gifts: lessons learned and memories of good times. Treasure the memories with all their charm. Learn the lessons, even the hard ones. But don't linger in yesterday. Like a vapor, it has vanished, making way for what's really important: the new day that is dawning. Accept the gift of the past and move on.

Father, thank You for my yesterdays, even the tough ones.
I've learned so much about myself, my journey, my actions
and reactions. I'll take what I'm meant to take from
yesterday—the lessons, the memories—but set
my sights on forward thinking. Amen.

337

The Present

Therefore do not worry about tomorrow, for tomorrow will worry about itself. Each day has enough trouble of its own.
MATTHEW 6:34 NIV

Today. Twenty-four hours of possibilities. A day where you can ask for forgiveness for the sins of yesterday and sit in God's presence, listening for His voice for guidance. A day when nothing else matters, not the worries associated with tomorrow's bills, not the what-ifs related to your job, not the concerns about where your health journey might be taking you. Today is a gift, for it causes you to stop and focus on what's directly in front of you. It doesn't tug you back and forth, to and fro. It pauses. It says, "Stay here awhile and settle in. Find peace in the midst of the storm." What is God speaking to your heart today? Have you truly let go of yesterday that you might find the gift that is directly in front of you? Thank God for the gift of today.

Father, thank You for the reminder that I'm called to live in today not yesterday. I don't want to go back, Lord. There are too many painful moments I'd rather forget. While it is still today, draw me close, Father. Let's spend precious moments together. Amen.

338

The Future

For I know the plans I have for you, declares the Lord,
plans for welfare and not for evil, to give
you a future and a hope.
JEREMIAH 29:11 ESV

Don't you just love the word *future*? It sings with possibility! The future is out there, beckoning, wishing you well. It's filled with surprises and opportunities, ready to pounce, like a sunrise inching its way above the horizon. Best of all, it's yours for the taking. So don't get bogged down with yesterday. Don't forget to praise God for today. But point yourself in the direction of tomorrow that hope might rise up in your heart. When you're excited about what's coming, you see life as an adventure. What adventures are you anticipating most? Do you trust God to take you there? He's ready to lead even now.

Lord, I've learned plenty of lessons from yesterday's mistakes.
I've learned to live in the present and to absorb all that
the day has to offer. But I'm excited about tomorrow
because I sense wonderful things are coming.
Thank You in advance, Father. Amen.

Wisdom

If any of you lacks wisdom, you should ask God,
who gives generously to all without finding
fault, and it will be given to you.
JAMES 1:5 NIV

You can study all your life and still not acquire wisdom. In fact, you can get your college degree, even your master's or PhD, and still not have wisdom. Sometimes very smart people make goofy mistakes due to lack of wisdom. They're loaded with knowledge but don't know how to balance it because wisdom is lacking. So where does wisdom come from? Why don't all people, educated or not, have a healthy dose of it? Wisdom comes from walking in relationship with God. It begins with hearing His voice and following His lead. Even the smallest child can walk in wisdom if she's listening to her heavenly Father. So lean in close. Get His perspective. That's what wisdom is, after all—God-perspective. And sure, go to school. Learn all you can. Gain knowledge. But remember that knowledge without wisdom won't take you very far.

I get it, Lord. I can acquire knowledge by studying. I gain
wisdom by walking close to You and emulating Your actions.
I want to be more like You, Father. Help me grow in
wisdom and stature as I draw close to You. Amen.

340

Resourcefulness

And when they had eaten their fill, he told his disciples,
"Gather up the leftover fragments, that nothing may be lost."
JOHN 6:12 ESV

She's resourceful. She knows how to make something out of nothing. Well, almost nothing. She uses bits of this and that to come up with amazing creations—foods you've never heard of, craft items you've never seen before. She also knows how to use tiny bits of money to pull off major events. Folks marvel at her ability to pull rabbits out of her hat. She's resourceful, all right, and you want to learn her tricks. So you watch carefully. You see how frugal she is, how she shops for the best deals. You watch as she borrows instead of buys, barters instead of spends, and stretches every dollar as far as she's able. She's a gift, this resourceful gal, and you're learning as fast as you can.

Lord, I need to be more resourceful. Thanks for placing
people in my path who lead by example. I'm watching!
I'm learning! May I stretch every dollar and become a
wise steward of what You've given me, Father. Amen.

341

Aging

Gray hair is a crown of glory;
it is gained in a righteous life.
PROVERBS 16:31 ESV

Aging is a gift. It's a sign that you're still alive and kicking, that you have time left with those you love. Every gray hair, every wrinkle, every age spot is also a sign that you've lived, you've loved, you've experienced life to the fullest. Best of all, you still have a purpose for living. You have something to offer those who are younger—stories of tenacity and joy, tales of overcoming obstacles. So don't look at the future with pain or fear. Don't worry about what tomorrow holds or how many years you have left. Instead, look to Jesus, the Author and perfecter of your faith. If He's able to count all of those gray hairs on your head and the tiny crevices where wrinkles are forming, surely He also knows the number of your days.

I won't fight it anymore, Lord. Who cares if my wrinkles make
my face look softer and gray hairs peek through? I will wear
my age spots like a badge of honor. I'm not ashamed of a life
well-lived, Father. Thank You for the reminder that I'm still
here, I still have purpose. I praise You for every breath. Amen.

Naps

I lie down and sleep; I wake again,
*because the L*ORD *sustains me.*
PSALM 3:5 NIV

～

Some days you just need a nap. Your eyelids are weighted down, begging to be closed. So you give in. You close the blinds in an attempt to block the sunlight streaming in from outside and then crawl between the covers. A last-minute glance at your cell phone reminds you that you'd better set an alarm. Otherwise you might sleep right through dinnertime and on through the night. Alarm now set, you rest your head against the pillows and allow your cares to fade away as sleep settles in—beautiful, glorious sleep. When you awake from your nap, you're a bit confused. Is it morning, afternoon, or night? Slivers of sunlight peek through the closed blinds, a reminder that the day isn't quite over yet. As you kick back the covers and swing your legs over the edge of the bed, peace settles over you. That nap was just what you needed, a free gift, yours for the taking. A little stretch follows, and then you're up and at 'em once again, ready to pick up the kids from school or fix dinner for your family. Ah, but what a glorious refresher, that wonderful nap!

* * *

Lord, I love naps. To be perfectly honest, I love sleeping
no matter the time of day. Thank You for the reminder
that naps are a gift, one I'm meant to enjoy.
I praise You for times of rest, Father. Amen.

343

Heaven

And if I go and prepare a place for you, I will come again and will take you to myself, that where I am you may be also.
JOHN 14:3 ESV

You've heard stories all your life. Streets of gold. Mansions of splendor. Gates of pearl. Angels singing. Elders worshipping. All of creation doing what they were born to do—celebrating eternity with their Creator. Sounds amazing, doesn't it? Perhaps the finest thing about heaven is that God wants you to see it all for yourself. In fact, He's so keen on you spending eternity with Him in heaven that He sent His Son, Jesus, to die on the cross for you to ensure your entrance into this amazing afterlife. Sure, you still have a lot of living to do here on Planet Earth. But the day will come when heaven will be your home. What a day that will be! Aren't you looking forward to the gift of heaven?

Father, I'm looking forward to heaven. I can't help but wonder, what will it look like, smell like, feel like? What sort of music will I hear? Will I eat food? If so, what kind? Who will I see when I get there? Friends who passed before me? Parents and grandparents? The anticipation is building as I imagine what it will be like, Lord. Thank You for including me in this great plan. Amen.

344

Peace

And the peace of God, which transcends all understanding,
will guard your hearts and your minds in Christ Jesus.
PHILIPPIANS 4:7 NIV

～

It doesn't make a bit of sense. Your stomach should be in knots.
Your head should be pounding. You should be pacing the room,
frantic. Instead, you're calm, cool, and collected. Most interesting,
because you've been through a real shaking, something that
would've taken down even the toughest person. It's almost as if
someone has set guard over your heart to protect you from the
pain of the situation. What you're feeling transcends anything
you've felt before. It's a supernatural impartation of peace as
only the Holy Spirit could give. You're cocooned in His comfort
and have every assurance that He's looking out for you. So rest
easy. Enjoy the peace that passes understanding, and thank
God for this amazing gift.

Lord, so many times I fret. I end up feeling so worked up
and agitated. I'm amazed by this peaceful feeling that
has settled over me. I can't explain it, but I'm so grateful
for it, Father. Thank You, Holy Spirit, for Your
divine comfort and peace. Amen.

345

Debt-Free Living

Owe no one anything, except to love each other,
for the one who loves another has fulfilled the law.
ROMANS 13:8 ESV

You've played the game before—robbing Peter to pay Paul. You've let debt run up, so you know the chokehold and the fear. Sure, you didn't do it on purpose, but it happened, and you had to pay the piper (literally). Not this time though. This time you're going a different route. You've decided to live within your means. No more drowning in debt. No more purchases you can't afford. From this point on, you work with a carefully constructed plan, one bent on giving you a life and a future, one free from unnecessary worries and/or calls from debt collectors. It's a challenge, but totally worth it. After all, is there any greater gift than debt-free living? That amazing sense of relief when you owe nothing? Perhaps you're not quite there yet. Today is the perfect day to start. Give yourself the gift of living within your means, and then watch as God brings peace to pave each step of the way.

Lord, I don't care for debt. I want to enjoy the freedom that
debt-free living can bring. Help me, I pray. Give me the
courage to say no to the things I don't really need and
the tenacity to stick with a life-giving plan.
I trust You, Father. Amen.

Your Favorite Fragrance

But thanks be to God, who in Christ always leads us in
triumphal procession, and through us spreads the
fragrance of the knowledge of him everywhere.
2 CORINTHIANS 2:14 ESV

It almost makes you giddy. You smell it and go weak in the knees. Maybe it's your favorite perfume. Or the smell of coffee. Or movie theater popcorn. Or Christmas candles. You're definitely partial to particular scents like cinnamon or birthday cake. But why do they affect you like they do? Some scents bring back memories of childhood. The smell of burgers cooking on the outside grill. The scent of fall leaves. The fresh smell of clothes straight from the dryer after tumbling around with the fabric softener sheet. Scents can comfort, soothe, and even bring joy. The gift of smell is one of the finest. Can you imagine how boring food would be without the ability to smell it? Today, pause to drink in several of the yummy scents around you as you're cooking and/or getting ready for the day. Then thank God for the sense of smell.

* * *

Thank You, Lord, for the sense of smell. It's one of my
favorites. Help me to pause and pay attention when
those amazing scents are wafting over me. I want to
take note of every little thing, I pray. Amen.

347

Recovery

Therefore, if anyone is in Christ, he is a new creation.
The old has passed away; behold, the new has come.
2 CORINTHIANS 5:17 ESV

~

The accident took a toll on her body. The doctors said it would take a long time to recover. Thank God, she pulled through. The cancer diagnosis left him hanging by a thread. You didn't know if he would make it, but somehow he miraculously survived and is now in remission. All around you, friends and loved ones have their recovery stories. You have a few of your own as well. The body's ability to rehabilitate itself, healing from the inside out, is remarkable. More than just recovering from a scratch, a broken bone, or a minor surgery, the human body is capable of pulling back from the abyss. What a remarkable God we serve, who created us with healing capabilities. He's placed us inside these amazing bodies, which regenerate as He directs. Such an amazing gift!

. . . .

Father, when I see all my friends and family have endured,
I marvel that so many have pulled through. There have been
some close calls, Lord. For the ones who've recovered, I thank
You. For those who are currently recovering, I pray for
healing. You've done wondrous work, Lord. Amen.

348

Close Calls

Be sober-minded; be watchful. Your adversary the devil prowls around like a roaring lion, seeking someone to devour.
1 PETER 5:8 ESV

Have you ever paused to think about all of the close calls in your life? Remember that time an eighteen-wheeler changed lanes, almost hitting you? And the time a fire swept through your county, barely missing your property? Remember that instance where the doctor felt sure you had a serious illness, but you later discovered he was wrong? If you took a look at every time the Lord has spared you of something catastrophic, chances are pretty good you could make quite a list. Today, pause to think through your close calls, then begin to praise God for His protection, provision, and healing. The enemy might be working overtime to take you down, but you have an army of angels on your side, ready to swing into action. Those close calls are really a gift because they remind you God isn't through with you yet. There's more ahead for you.

* * *

I've had so many near misses, Lord. The enemy has worked hard to bring me down. But You've protected me, Father, and led me to this point. I know I can trust You no matter what comes my way. Praise You for that protection! Amen.

349

Comfort Food

*Jesus said to them, "I am the bread of life;
whoever comes to me shall not hunger,
and whoever believes in me shall never thirst."*
JOHN 6:35 ESV

Mama knew just what foods made you feel better when you were sick—chicken soup, homemade bread, pudding. . .or anything else your heart desired. Grilled cheese sandwiches. French toast. Homemade chocolate pudding. Coconut pie. Everyone has their own list of foods that bring comfort. To many, chocolate is the perfect elixir. To others, sour or bitter foods hit the spot. Today, as you stop to think about your own particular comfort foods, why not take the time to thank God for providing them? He cares even about the little things that bring you pleasure. (Why else would He have created the cocoa bean?) He's also provided chefs with the God-given ability to create delicacies out of His creations. What a gift!

*Father, I love comfort foods. Some days I just need a bowl
of chicken soup or homemade bread. Thank You for
creating the foundational foods—grains, proteins,
fruits, and chocolate—so I can enjoy
these little luxuries. Amen.*

350

The Quiet Evening Hours

Have you not known? Have you not heard? The LORD is the
everlasting God, the Creator of the ends of the earth. He does
not faint or grow weary; his understanding is unsearchable.
ISAIAH 40:28 ESV

You've had a long day. You were up before the sun and took
care of things around the house. Prepped kids for school. Went
to work. Shuffled the kids off to sports practice. Came home to
a messy house. Fixed dinner. Picked up while the kids bathed.
Did a couple loads of laundry. Filled the dishwasher. Then
collapsed in an easy chair when they tumbled into bed. Now,
with only the hum of the dishwasher and a quiet conversation
from the television, you're ready to relax. In fact, a bubble bath
sounds good. So you fill the tub, settle back, and do your best
to put the day behind you. There will be more laundry to fold
when you get out, but for now you simply need to enjoy the
stillness of the evening. It is today's finest gift, one you plan to
take full advantage of!

Lord, I confess. I get so tired. The days seem so long, Lord,
that I wonder if I'll make it through. Then those quiet hours
of the evening come, and I sense Your peace settling over me.
The sun has set. The day is almost done. And I'm finally
free to just be. Thank You for meeting me
in those moments, Father. Amen.

Medical Advances

Is there no balm in Gilead? Is there no physician there?
Why then has the health of the daughter of my
people not been restored?
JEREMIAH 8:22 ESV

She's been given the worst possible news. Things seem impossible. Just when all hope seems lost, a new treatment is offered. She takes it and prays for the best possible outcome. He's at the end of his rope, his body isn't responding to the meds, and things are looking bleak. The doctor switches gears, changes up his meds, and things begin to improve. In this fast-paced world, things are always changing, morphing, growing. Advances are happening every single day. Lives are being impacted for the better as scientists and doctors work together to fight diseases like cancer, diabetes, heart disease, and more. Aren't you glad you live in a day and age when advances like these can take place, when hope is always on the horizon? Today think about a friend who's going through a medical crisis. Pray specifically that God will send just the right doctors, medicines, and/or advice to bring healing.

* * *

Thank You, God, for medical advances. Every day a new treatment, a new plan, a new medicine, a new way to treat naturally. I'm so grateful for each advancement, Father, and thrilled to be living in a day and age when medicine has the power to save lives. Today I lift up the scientists, doctors, and pharmacologists who are working hand in hand to eradicate diseases. Thank You, Lord. Amen.

Upbeat People

Finally, brothers, whatever is true, whatever is honorable,
whatever is just, whatever is pure, whatever is lovely,
whatever is commendable, if there is any excellence,
if there is anything worthy of praise,
think about these things.
PHILIPPIANS 4:8 ESV

They're always thinking about the best not the worst. They have a way of turning a blah day into a fun one. These are the people you want to be around because they're fun, confirming, and hopeful. When you're down in the dumps, just a few minutes with one of these friends will have you laughing and forgetting your troubles. Upbeat people are a gift! So what about you? Would people say you're upbeat? Do you have that personality others are drawn to? Even if you're a shy person, you can still exude positivity and encouragement. If you're not naturally jubilant, just ask the Lord to give you a double dose of joy. There! Doesn't that feel good?

Lord, I love to be around upbeat people. They can turn any
event into a party. Help me stay positive and upbeat so
that I can encourage others, Lord. I want to
turn their frowns upside down! Amen.

353

Furnishings

*And when the hour came, he reclined at table,
and the apostles with him.*
LUKE 22:14 ESV

That comfy sofa with its worn cushions. That breakfast table, stained from your toddler's juice. That mattress, perfectly fitted to your body. These items and so many more in your home might seem commonplace to you, but they are gifts meant to comfort and sustain you. Every piece of furniture you own—whether fine or flawed—tells a story. The dresser from your grandmother. The coffee table you purchased from your best friend at a garage sale. That recliner your husband refuses to give up. These stories are part of the family tapestry now, adding color and texture to your life. So go on. Settle down onto that lumpy chair. Tighten the legs of the dining room chairs for the umpteenth time. Your furniture is a gift, one that keeps you from spending your days on the floor.

I'll admit it, Lord. Sometimes I envy those who have nicer things. I want newer, better, sturdier. Maybe that day will come, but until it does, I choose to praise You for providing what I need, even if it's not always what I would have handpicked. I'm grateful for Your provision, Lord. Amen.

354

Christmas Season

*For God so loved the world that he gave his one
and only Son, that whoever believes in him
shall not perish but have eternal life.*
JOHN 3:16 NIV

Jingle bells. Colorful decorations at the mall. Choir presentations at church. Carolers at your door. 'Tis the Christmas season, and you love everything about it. This amazing season takes you back to your childhood, when you waited with breathless anticipation to see what presents would land under the tree, when you wondered if you would get that new bike or tablet. Now you're the one planning the surprises for the little ones in your life, and you're having a blast! Prepping for the big day is so much fun. In fact, you're enjoying it even more than the kids are. So go ahead. Get in the Christmas spirit. Enjoy the season of happiness and goodwill. It's an amazing gift!

*Father, what a joyous season. There's so much to look forward
to. I love everything about it. May I always carry that childlike
anticipation as I share the good news of what You did that
very first Christmas, Lord. It's the greatest story ever! Amen.*

355

Christmas Decorations

*Splendor and majesty are before him;
strength and joy are in his place.*
1 CHRONICLES 16:27 ESV

⁓

That special ornament your daughter made in kindergarten.
Those colorful, twinkling lights. That train under the tree. The
singing Santa on the mantel. The miniature Christmas village
on the hall table. All of these decorations bring a smile to your
face and put you in the mood for Christmas. Whether you're the
sort to "deck the halls" or not, you have to admit that a house
filled with Christmas decor puts you in the mood to sing carols
and drink hot cocoa. And you can't deny that all the trappings
of Christmas are fun, as long as you keep them in their place,
remembering that the season is really about Jesus' birth. So
what's keeping you? Pull those boxes down from the attic. Go
buy that tree. Hang lights on your house. 'Tis the season!

*Father, I love the Christmas season. I do my best to keep
Christ at the center of it all, but I can't deny that I love the
colors of the decorations and the festive way they make
me feel. Thank You for the gift of Christmas
and for the colors of the season. Amen.*

356

Baking

*As each has received a gift, use it to serve one another,
as good stewards of God's varied grace.*
1 PETER 4:10 ESV

❧

Don't you just love baked goods (and those who bake them)?
Hot apple pie. Angel food cake. Peanut butter cookies. Chocolate
chip scones. Homemade cinnamon rolls. Hot bread slathered
with butter. These are just a few of the tasty delights a baker
pulls from her oven. She pours her heart and soul into each offering. There's something so magical about mixing flour, sugar,
eggs, and vanilla to concoct cakes, cookies, and so much more.
The ingredients transform as they heat up, morphing from one
thing into another. The oven itself seems to have special powers,
for the things that come out of it are unparalleled. How good
of God to inspire bakers to create yummy delights. May more
bakers receive inspiration so we might all enjoy their wares not
just during the Christmas season but year-round.

*Lord, I'm grateful for bakers and baked goods. I have my
favorites, of course, but all of those yummy warm cookies,
cupcakes, and scones are pure delight. They are a gift, one I
don't mind sampling again and again. Thank You! Amen.*

357

Christmas Gifts

Thanks be to God for his inexpressible gift!
2 CORINTHIANS 9:15 ESV

❧

Packages wrapped with ribbons and bows. Name tags for every carefully wrapped gift. A majestic tree hovering over the stacked presents. Children's eyes wide with wonder as the gifts make their way to their respective owners. The tearing of paper, the ripping of bows, the clamoring for scissors to cut open plastic packaging. Inside, gifts you've handpicked ready to be revealed. Is there anything more exciting than opening presents together on Christmas morning? Sure, the house ends up a bit messy, but who cares? The squeals of delight, the beaming faces, the toothless grins. . .they make it all worthwhile. Whether you're the parent or the grandparent, or you're looking back to special memories from childhood, gifts under the tree are pure delight.

Father, I love Christmas gifts. So much planning goes into every single one. I buy them with TLC for each little boy and girl, each friend, each loved one. And I receive them with equal joy. These gifts mean so much to me, Lord. Thank You for each one, for each represents someone I adore. Amen.

358

The Ultimate Gift

While they were there, the time came for the baby to be born, and she gave birth to her firstborn, a son. She wrapped him in cloths and placed him in a manger, because there was no guest room available for them.
LUKE 2:6–7 NIV

During the Christmas rush, it's easy to get caught up in the chaos. A mad dash to the mall. A quick trip to the toy department of your favorite store. A few more items purchased online. Decorating the house. Planning the Christmas Day menu. Cooking. Baking. Looking at lights. Watching Christmas movies. Whew! Things can get crazy! May we never forget that Christmas, as magical and childlike as it is, is really about the birth of our Savior, Jesus Christ. All of our celebrations would be for naught if not for Him. Today, as you think about all you've been given this holiday season, remember that the greatest gift of all came wrapped in swaddling clothes, a tiny baby boy in a manger. He grew up, lived a life worthy of emulating, and then died for all humankind. We'll never receive a more precious gift.

Father, thank You for the ultimate gift—Your Son. I don't know how You did it, Lord, giving Him up for over thirty-three years. And yet, He came willingly. . .for me. How can I ever express my thanks, Father? This is the most amazing gift I have ever received, and I'm so grateful. Amen.

A Good Book

*As for these four youths, God gave them learning
and skill in all literature and wisdom, and Daniel had
understanding in all visions and dreams.*
DANIEL 1:17 ESV

It's been a long week. You're tired, ready to rest, wanting to lose yourself in a good story. The pages call out to you, begging to be turned. That perfect cover draws like a magnet. The author is new to you, but you're willing to give her a chance. So you settle in with a cup of tea, ready to be entertained, swept away by the story. The book does not disappoint. Before long, you're caught up in the lives of the characters, drawn into the setting, and wondering where the plotline will take you next. You stay awake long into the night, turning page after page, starting chapter after chapter, not caring about the time. Only when you awake groggy a few hours later do you regret the decision to keep reading. Even then, you wouldn't go back and do things differently. A good book is a gift, a powerful tool in your hands. It can transport you, lift you out of your doldrums, and shift your focus. So go ahead—reach for that next one. You know you want to!

*Father, thank You for good books. They are such a blessing
in my life. Bless the many authors I love, Lord,
and inspire them to write even more. Amen.*

360

Siblings

We ought always to give thanks to God for you, brothers,
as is right, because your faith is growing abundantly,
and the love of every one of you for one another is increasing.
2 THESSALONIANS 1:3 ESV

That pesky older brother. That precocious little sister. That squealing baby in the crib. What a handful they used to be. Now that you're all grown, they've morphed into friends, mentors, companions, not just during the holidays but year-round. You don't know what you'd do without them, in fact. You pray you'll never have to know. There's a sense of comfort and familiarity when you're around your siblings. They have your back when you need defending, they share the burdens when you need a shoulder, and they lift you up in prayer when you're unsure of the road ahead. Best of all, they're a part of you—physically, emotionally, psychologically. You are family. What an amazing gift!

Lord, I'm so grateful for my siblings today. Oh, what a gift
they are! Some are related by blood. Others are siblings of
the heart, adopted into my life in a way that brings joy
and comfort. Thank You for surrounding me with kin,
Father. I praise You for family. Amen.

Old Photographs

So God created man in his own image, in the image of God he created him; male and female he created them.
GENESIS 1:27 ESV

～

It's just an old black-and-white photo with frayed edges, so why does it tug on your heart with such force? You give it a closer look. Mama's eyes are twinkling, and Papa has that crooked grin of his. There you are, a precocious youngster, standing between them. Your hand-sewn outfit causes your heart to swell with memories of Mama, and the hole in the knee brings back a vivid recollection of digging in the dirt with your brother, who stands to your left in the photo. In the background stands the house you grew up in, complete with that broken shutter on the front window. The tree you used to climb made it into the photo too, along with the hedges you and your best friend hid in. Yes, it's just a picture, but it has evoked bittersweet memories that bring tears to your eyes and a smile to your lips. What a gift old photos are. They transport you to a simpler time, lift your heart, and make you oh-so-grateful to the Lord for all He's given you.

. . . .

Father, thank You for the photos of my past. They've captured glimpses of my life, preserved for posterity. Some are easy to look at. Others, not so much. But I'll take it all, Lord, the good and the bad, for You saw me through it all, one snapshot at a time. Amen.

362

Microwaves

Give us this day our daily bread.
MATTHEW 6:11 ESV

Ah, the convenience of modern living. Our meals can arrive at the table in two minutes or less, thanks to inventions like the microwave. White, fluffy kernels of popcorn can rise in joyous mounds inside a paper bag in just three minutes. Cakes can be baked in coffee cups in five minutes or less. Meat can be thawed in time for supper. Sometimes we forget what life was like before the microwave came on the scene. Grandma kept a plate of food warm by covering it in foil and putting it in the oven. She softened butter by leaving it out on the counter. She made the filling for her chocolate pies on the stovetop, praying she wouldn't scorch it. These processes took a long time, but she knew no other way. You, on the other hand? You have options. And with this crazy-busy life you lead, the microwave is a partner and friend.

Lord, thank You for modern marvels like the microwave.
I'm grateful for options, Father, and for the convenience
of getting something done in a hurry. Amen.

363

History

For whatever was written in former days was written for our instruction, that through endurance and through the encouragement of the Scriptures we might have hope.
ROMANS 15:4 ESV

They say hindsight is 20/20. History teaches us many of the lessons we need to learn in life. From the mistakes of those who walked before us, we learn what not to do. From their successes, we are inspired to do our best. As this year draws to a close, look back over your "history." Examine this year with a critical eye. What lessons have you learned? What will you do again? What will you avoid? The ability to scrutinize where you've been is a gift, one necessary for moving forward. God wants you to learn from your mistakes, dust yourself off, and point yourself toward the next year. Great things are coming. Are you ready for them?

Father, I'll admit I've done quite a few things wrong this year. I don't have the best "history" lesson, but I've learned from my mistakes. I know what not to repeat. Thank You for the lessons, Lord. I'm still on a learning curve, but You're a gentle teacher. I know You'll stick with me as I move forward into the New Year, and we'll do great things together! Amen.

364

Insight

I have counsel and sound wisdom;
I have insight; I have strength.
PROVERBS 8:14 ESV

～

You can see beyond what you see with your eyes. You have insight into problems and situations that leave others perplexed. There's only one reason you have this special knack for seeing what others can't—you're tuned in to what the Holy Spirit is telling you. Your ears are wide open, and so is your heart. This is going to come in very handy as you turn the pages of the calendar and move into the New Year. There are exciting things coming, and you'll need to know how to handle them. That's okay. . .you're wise. You seek good counsel. You have insight and strength. You're prepared for the road ahead because you've taken your walk with God seriously. Great things are coming around the bend!

. . . .

Lord, thank You for insight. I love having Your vision for the
road ahead. I can sense that amazing things are around the
bend, and I can't wait to see what You plan to do through me.
I'll do my best to grow in wisdom and stature in this New Year,
Lord. What fun we'll have, walking hand in hand. Amen.

365

The Finish Line

I have fought the good fight,
I have finished the race,
I have kept the faith.
2 TIMOTHY 4:7 ESV

You've kept going, even with obstacles in your way. You've faced tough days, hard conversations, bumps in relationships. But you're not the sort to stop just short of the finish line. You're going to keep going until the year has come to an end. Then you'll pick yourself up again and dive into the next year with hope leading the way. Most importantly, you won't give up on your faith even when others around you are waffling. You want to finish well. And that's what God wants for you too. He wants the seasons to draw to their natural conclusion and new ones to begin. So don't look at where you've been. Don't get hung up on emotional turmoil or relationship woes. Keep your eye on the prize. The finish line is calling your name.

Father, I want to end well. I aim myself toward the finish line
and determine in my heart to hit it. May I bring honor to You
as I complete the tasks set before me. I need Your help,
Lord. Give me strength, courage, and tenacity
to get this job done. Amen.

SCRIPTURE INDEX

If You Liked This Book,
You'll Want to Take a Look at...

By Still Waters

Here are 365 devotions that will quiet and refresh your soul. Encouraging inspiration and insights from scripture offer daily reminders that God is not only present but also invites you, His beloved daughter, to come away with Him to rest by still waters—to be restored, comforted, spiritually fed, and assured of His perfect love.

Paperback / 978-1-68322-456-3 / $7.99

You Are Loved

Bestselling author Darlene Sala seeks to encourage Christian women with these 90 lovely devotional readings. In *You Are Loved*, readers will see God's heart for them, His concern for the trials and struggles they face, and that He is always watching, listening, and loving.

Paperback / 978-1-68322-589-8 / $4.99